A Crack in the Sidewalk

Tarringo T. Vaughan

PublishAmerica
Baltimore

© 2011 by Tarringo T. Vaughan.
All rights reserved. No part of this book may be reproduced, stored in a retrieval system or transmitted in any form or by any means without the prior written permission of the publishers, except by a reviewer who may quote brief passages in a review to be printed in a newspaper, magazine or journal.

First printing

PublishAmerica has allowed this work to remain exactly as the author intended, verbatim, without editorial input.

Softcover 978-1-4626-5439-0
PUBLISHED BY PUBLISHAMERICA, LLLP
www.publishamerica.com
Baltimore

Printed in the United States of America

Table of Contents

I As This Day Begins 15

   Magic 17

   As This Day Begins 19

   This Simple Amazing 21

   A Crack In The Sidewalk 23

   Imagine 25

   The Here And Now 27

   The Nature Of Beauty 29

   Soon September 30

   October Skies 32

   Rue Sainte-Catherine 34

   Always 37

   Across Mulberry Street 38

   One Moment 40

   Poetic Rhapsody 42

   Something Said The Wind 43

   It Came To Me In A Dream 44

   Often 46

   Dreaming With Open Eyes 47

   Wind Chimes 49

Footprint Of Discovery 50

Thoughts Swirling With The Wind 51

Nauset Beach 53

There Again… 55

To Spring 56

To The Bird Who Sings The Morning Song 57

To The Tree That Once Stood Strong 58

Florentine Gardens 60

II The Long Everlasting 63

Metaphors 65

To An Empty Chair 67

Nothing/ness 69

A Place I Used To Call Home 71

The Long Everlasting 73

Coffee Shop Flyers 74

Nostalgia 77

What Happened In Harlem 78

A Simple Ginsberg 80

This Side Of Bukowski 83

Off The Corner Of Main Street 85

Dining In Connecticut 87

Washington Square 90

III. Through These Eyes Only 93

Genius 95

Through These Eyes Only 97

1924 99

One Day In 1960 101

Miss Jackee 103

Let Him Be 105

The Young Americans 106

Niche 108

Our Playground 109

IV. The Evidence Of Existence 111

Brilliance 113

Empty Streets 114

Battle Scars 115

The Evidence Of Existence 116

The Lyrics Of Her Song 118

Broken High Heels 120

She Use To Be That Girl 122

One Man's Own 124

The Thoughts Of Curiosity 126

Mission Hill 128

Grandaddy's Song 130

V. Poetry For Progress 133

Diversity 135

2:26 A.M 137

A City Of Dreams 138

Every City Has A Ghetto 140

Of Life's Complexity 142

Dangerfield 143

Street Corners And Hustlers 145

Streets of Success 147

A Poem For Progress 149

I Have Dreams 151

Miss Parks 153

The Roads Of Selma, 1963 154

The Sidewalks of Yesterday 155

VI. Awakened 157

Therapy 159

Awakened 160

SiLeNcE 161

Outcast 162

On The Random Road Of Confusion 163

10:53 P.M. 164

Ashes 166

The Last Tomorrow 167

Life's Recipe. 168

The Light Of Sanity 169

The Timeless 170

Street of Consequences 171

People 172

Break Of Dawn 173

VII. The Adventures Of Mr. Poetry 175

Mr .Poetry I 177

Mr. Poetry II 179

Mr. Poetry III 181

Mr. Poetry IV 183

Mr. Poetry V 185

Mr. Poetry VI 187

Mr. Poetry VII 189

Mr. Poetry VIII 191

"To me, every hour of the day and night is an unspeakably perfect miracle."
— Walt Whitman

Dedicated To The Footprints Of Every Soul

I As This Day Begins

"There is so much life out there as I watch and prepare to join this screenplay with no stage directions."

__Magic__

I walk through this world in awe.

   Tattooed sidewalks of flawed granite smothered by footprints of graffiti connecting generations of magicians give off the aroma of something amazing. There are days I wonder how we came to be. There are days I try to imagine who made the sky the perfect shade of blue on gray days of rain and who made the ocean waves the elegant force of gentle rage. I wonder how flowers came to be the scent of comfort and the symbols passion, beauty and sadness; I wonder how emotion has become that great potion of transient tears connecting all of us through the many languages we communicate. Ever since I was a little boy I've admired and been held in a sensual but rugged curiosity of how this all came to be. Maybe this existence is nothing but an illusion but an illusion from what? Is our reality really a dream or just a discovery of all the possibilities…*out there?*

We live inside a journey of invention.

   I have come to realize that it is our minds that are magic. The processes of intelligence we exhibit is fascinating. There have been those who have cured by mixing science with healing and those who have built tombs with hands of genetic precision. There have been those who have written the history of future mankind with metaphors perfectly intertwined into the masterpiece of translation and there have been those who have imagined the technology of imagery and brilliance. But what is my magic on this wonderland? Sometimes I think it is my own vision as I can see things others may ignore to see but most times I feel it is my interpretation as through my poetic understanding I am able to become a witness outside my own stanzas of existence because as poets we can be anywhere at any time; we can be many places at once and turn simple objects into complex fountains of description. We can fool the eyes with hidden meaning and hold them blindfolded with clarity. We invent through our pens and with the wordplay of endless thoughts and observations. The many questions of this world are the answers we create through the written language of magic.

As This Day Begins

The sky yawns as the sun light parachutes
down upon my eyes lifting me up to a new dawn.
As I rise up to my window I see birds,

many birds

playing hop scotch on shadowed sidewalks
mystified by naked trees and aging light posts

dimmed

by blue skies that are smiling down upon
the traffic's roar. A heavy set man is running
five minutes late towards his transportation
but the bus driver plays blind and speeds off

looking behind to see a middle finger
honking wildly at a right blinker that turns
down a hill and disappears in a fume of acceleration.
And further down the street there is a celebration
as parents are high fiving school busses with their joy
while their children are waving and giggling

at headlights jogging off to workplaces

desired and *undesired.* A police man is spying
on grumpy motorists sipping **Starbuc**k lattés
and barley paying attention to traffic stops screaming
at them to slow down.

A young Black woman walks and stands
next to the heavy set man who is now fifteen minutes
late. She nods hello with her eyes
and he says "fuck off" with his body language.

The two mingle with their backs turned
towards each other

gazing in opposite directions
with different starts to this same day.

So much life out there as I watch and prepare
to join the screenplay with no stage directions.

Anything can happen out there in the world and any little
mishap can change the emotion of this day.
I'm just thinking: who will be watching me
and what will they be writing

as this day begins.

<u>This Simple Amazing</u>

I did not want to write today but my mind cannot help
but scribble the images around me as I wander
this landscape of exposed mysteries.

Leaves of golden brown and slightly reddish orange
tickle my muddy sneakers with a splashing kiss
as I trample them with the whistle of my walk.

      I did not want to write today…but

this path glistens as those birds over there by the hedges are humming
greedily for my attention. They fly but slowly as they
perform for the audience of my eyes. They see me
and I'm humming as bird shit drops on the baldest spot
of my freshly shaved head.

    Fuck!

But then again this is the joy of living; the joy of existing
together with these other creatures who wander this never-ending
season of change.

It is this simple amazing that is making me smile
as I photograph the perfect nakedness of tree branches
that are waltzing with this wind; a wind that is playfully
tickling my eyelashes and is causing me to blink.

    I like this.

I like being a witness to this change as beauty
gives way to beauty and the earth hardens
but softens for new refreshing experiences and expeditions of life.

I don't mind that I am alone here as I am exploring
the cardiovascular system of inspiration. I did not want to write today
but the clouds are threatening me with a glimpse of winter
causing me to pull my hood over my head that is smudged
with bird shit from a cardinal.

    But it's good luck. They say.

And I believe it because I am a part of this
    (What shall I call it?)

    Formality?

I like originality better…so yeah I'll go with that.

I never saw such a huge cat.

A cat that is trying to escape my glance
by scattering behind half decayed logs and weeds
that seem to never die no matter how cold
the touch of mother nature's massage.

I told myself I didn't want to write today
but this time and the pure essence of inhaling
drips in ink from this wide open sky of limitless
exposure.

I'm tired of walking but I will never tire
of taking this all in. Right here

    in this simple amazing.

A Crack In The Sidewalk

It is but a perfect display of a flaw; a
formation in the cement upon which I
solidly stand.
Brush away the slight cough of sand
and there paved
unintentionally is something
to marvel.

History sculptured within millions
perhaps billons of endless
footsteps of comers and goers
stamped by smudges of dog shit
and sticky bubble gum
washed away by everyday spit
and tears in the form of rain
creating a slippery surface
of existence.

It is a reminder that I do not
walk on perfect ground but a ground
that indeed should be admired.

This crack in the sidewalk
with the small weed sprouting
from a dampened moss
is where passengers of life ride
as scavengers
 searching for pride

and it is where pain has found strength
and sadness has found laughter;
it is where history meets future

greeters as today
they are just strangers
roaming to destinations
of simply being.

For those who say step on a crack
and achieve years of bad luck
I say 'look you silly fucks',
it is only lucky to share the steps
of so many who have helped
create this flaw
of perfection.

<u>Imagine</u>

A mildly dented beer can is sitting on
the edge of sobriety. It stands still against
a shifting wind that is balancing its 'Budweiser' logo
on the surface of my vision; once twelve ounces
of substance now half full or half empty
depending on how the angle of the mind
stares down the circular blinking eye of tin.

Imagine where this can has been

Imagine the beauty in someone's unfinished booze
minding its own business on this cluttered sidewalk
filled with remnants of the night before. A stale must
lingers barely washed away by a slight cough

in the air

I wonder how it got there and I imagine

    Somewhere

the lips of an over partier is waking up hung-over
physically drained but much alive celebrating
another day of chances;

a chance to start new;
    a chance to witness brighter skies
        a chance to resurface in someone's eyes.

Because who knows what one more sip
would've conquered before the night's demise
or why this can was left there as an advertisement

of optimism.

This life is a prism of imaginations that connects
worlds that we wouldn't know existed otherwise
and as I stand here and fantasize and give life
to something meant to be stepped over or thrown away
I recognize…

That here I imagine

the significance of someone else's garbage
abandoned here on a public sidewalk
serving as an introduction to someone out there
who left it sitting here

to be written.

<u>The Here And Now</u>

These thoughts are dancing through the hollow
cylinder of my mind as translations of time

(paused)

 into the experience of being…a poet

and tomorrow has gone into extinction
as this moment has captured eternity's glass eye
where I see reflections of no escape
peering through windows scraped

      by the fingertips of yesterday.

Right here, right now I sit in the middle
of an empty room filled with crowds

      of inspiration.

They don't see me because they are absent
shadows of my surroundings.

A blind girl captures the fragrance of sight
as she feels her way through the aroma
of distant stares.

      She is amazed at their beauty

simplified in perfect fragments of…ignorance
as her description and movement is being
written by a stranger who knows her well.

Poetry is her brail and I read her brilliance
knowing her footprints will not fade
into tomorrow's disappearance.

And right here, right now I study
the sands of time as they blow wildly
through visions I've never been introduced to

    before.

The blind girl surrounded by the enigmas
who enhance their eye movement with every
step of her silence realize they are the blind ones

who are forgetting the importance

    of the now as they look forward

to a memory that will be forgotten
in the never promised winds of tomorrow

and I sit in a crowded room of emptied existence
with thoughts dancing through the hollow
cylinder of my mind frantically writing this all

    into a poem

blind of time.

The Nature Of Beauty

I stand here faithful to the wind
as birds clutch the sky with a smile;
the sadness in my heart descends
on the path of this joyous aisle;
and this is where your soul ascends
in the air of peaceful exile.

Your hands do echo down on me
from the spirit of heavens skies.
You are the fragrance of each tree
dancing through the sight of my cries
as in these surroundings I see
this nature's beauty through your eyes.

Soon September

Another summer begins its formation into hibernation
as this air sneezes a brisk morning dew onto shivering
car hoods and barefoot grass slightly covered
with the breeze of autumn. This is what a writer dreams;
this reality of nature's act of illusion—

>the cool smoothness of a liquid sky yawing
>its sunlight into windows grazed by a peppered fog;

the shadows of crows barking their arrogance on the top
of rusted steel fences polished by the dampness of these clouds.
I can smell these leaves as they begin to camouflage into syrupy brown
and a bright orange bringing out the deep burgundy
eyes of nearby rose bushes as crisp petals perfume

>transient sidewalk curbs with a lasting reminder
>of summers youth. I am alone here for a moment

watching the eyelids of dawn open to a new day; listening
to the sweetness of birds whistling conversations
of fascination; and feeling the shift of the season prepare
for a new awaking as the childhood of June has become

the adolescence of August and now September begins
its puberty. Time has begun its transcendence into a lapsed stillness
and I feel it as my mind dances here beneath the music
of aqua haze; a sky pleasantly whining from the womb
of summer

as soon September the day light will diminish into the sounds
of an early harvest and soon crumpled leaves will become
ballerinas twirled gently to a hardening ground

ready for the chilled champagne of October hue;

soon September the children will climb the bare branches
of earths many jungle gyms: trees standing as nudists
        clothed in the maple bark of autumns touch;

soon September this clarity will become the majestic kiss
of abstract temperatures with light misty eyed tears
raining gently on damp mornings like today,

        and soon September writers will share this choir
of harmonic poetry as a new season enters through fields
where illuminated thought radiates. Soon these surroundings
shall become something new

                as soon September arrives and a new inspiration
                will become alive.

October Skies

Autumn is crying on this shitty day
as October skies sprinkle a steady stream
of teardrops down upon the forecast
of dampened smiles.

Lazy clouds fraternize and are refusing
to give way to an impatient sun
that eventually parishes behind an overbearing
blanket of gray just as my eyes
are looking up through this fogged window
that parallels the warmth of my breathing;
the reflection of my awareness.

I don't want to go out there.

Because puddles are dancing to the tap of the winds
as flooded street sewers soak
hidden sidewalks that are tattooed
with mother's natures quilt of fallen leaves
that are serving as a foot mat for scurrying
strangers who are tracking their existence
on the floors of time.

I don't want to be out there,

as whistling winds are turning up the skirts
of frightened umbrellas exposing their steel brim legs
to the roar of the air.
And there is a bird flying near
that drops a load of good luck on a swerving car
with windshield wipers now waving
frantically for clarity.

But none of this is noticed by the young boy

splashing in puddles of adolescence
as the world is happening around him.
He is laughing as his goulashes clap
to the standing ovation of my flattery.

You know…only a poet would make a portrait
out of a shitty day;
only a poet would be giving life to those leaves
that have died and now are mourned by branches
left bare of their colorful coats of admiration;
and only a poet would see himself
in the childhood of innocence
as this all is happening.

I don't want to go out there, but I'm there.

As poetry's witness.

Not all October skies are beautiful,
they are sometimes teary and dreary;
they sometimes don't appear at all
but this day I am sitting in appreciation
of the inspiration that is happening within the many stories
out there; the many stories that are catching my attention

right here,
right now
in these mere minutes
of life

right here,
right now
(in these mere moments
of poetry.)

Rue Sainte-Catherine

I am mirrored as just another American
tourist in their eyes.
I have a crumpled upside down
map blindly guiding me towards a street sign
that reads *rue Sainte-Catherine* and right
through the amusement
of these Canadian natives who are
welcoming me to Montreal
with stares that giggle.

I feel like a stubborn ass
twirling around in the form
of a lost fool
because that's exactly what I am;
a lost fool
pampered with too much pride
to ask simple directions
back to familiarity,
not that any of this is familiar at all

But,
I have nothing but admiration
for the texture of this city,
even with the French slurs being
ushered my way, (or maybe
just my overactive paranoia), I'm walking
the steps of exhilaration as I'm
in awe of the richness
sprinkled throughout the historic
architecture of this city.

Just to be somewhere new,
to experience;

to inhale a different kind of air
refreshes who I am and all the little things
in life I take for granted.

Here's a little café at the corner
that reminds me of this little
place I used to go to back in the states,
it was called the Blue moon café
and I used to sit amongst the radiance
of dimmed lights with a soft bluesy music
that decorated the atmosphere with
a fragrance of escape.
It was my time to just explore
my mind and decipher
the nuances around me
in metaphoric phrases.

I never thought I would be standing
here, in the middle of a place
where people are walking by staring
at my reflection propelled from window
front of this place I've found myself
to be fond of.
This is a very free verse city--
thoughts just pop in your head here
and you have to go with it,
it's funny, I used to always think of Montreal
as a sonnet well organized in lyrical stanzas.

Inside I see lap top computers,
in front of faces to be admired;
postures and body language I recognize
without the need of translation.
I wonder what they are writing about?

Freelancers, writers…oh I know, poets!
I can spot a poet anywhere, even
in the midst of a city that does not
care what's on my mind.
To them I'm nothing but a cinquain:
five little lines clustered together
to form one big lost mess.

All of this; all of this going on right here
right now, the strange looks, the map
that makes no sense, the café sheltering
artists of the written word who are
staring out into the land of bullshit!
Yes it's all bullshit,
but bullshit to be captured
and remembered because
this is all poetry!
So let me open this door
sit down, grab a latte and write about
this bullshit.

Always

thinking...Always thinking about the many shades
of blue that clutter the sky. Sometimes I walk on perfectly
cracked brick sidewalks with my eyes lifted up high
wondering and dreaming about my purpose—the footprints
of my thoughts are finely paved on paper but a poets
words is only truly published when they filter the minds
of future generations. Always writing/ I am always writing
about the deep obscurities of self-definition. Sometimes
I write on the backs of strangers hoping my words
will inspire or change the way they decide to conquer
this world/hoping my experience can change a life
or cure a tear because we learn to breathe again
when a hidden familiarity of the heart stops and stare
reminding us that we are not alone/never alone
even when we stand stranded underneath puddles
of internal pain. Always searching/I am always searching
for new ways to create. Sometimes I feel my fingertips
are magicians as the words I write travel through
places I never knew existed/places within a poet's
observation and places out there—out there in a world
where destinations are fulfillments and realizations
are accomplishments—out there where literary freedom
is the balance between those who read and those who need
to be written. Always dreaming/I am always dreaming
while wide awake. There are times I open the eyes
of my life and see visions of history where past geniuses
still live in the heartbeat of an art that never fades/an art
passed through influential minds to be released
        and always be the translation of poetry.

Across Mulberry Street

Looking back through the history age, I walked alone
locked inside the mind of a loner traveling
daily back and forth on a path between home
and everything…out there/1994 I walked the windy
road of Mulberry Street over a thousand times and each
journey was different than the time before. There was
always a new texture from the sun as the
steady warmth energized the eyelids of buildings;
      there was always a different kind of obedience
painting the air with point tip tree branches; there was always
a calming silence whistling through the melody of the birds
and each day my eyes took on a new growth;

a growth I didn't recognize until I allowed my mind
to marinate within the time and tranquility of it all.
It was my human nature as a creative spectator to film
with thoughts and the energy of interpretation. I was eighteen
back then and just weeks away from graduating
my twelfth year of renewal and all I can remember is this walk
that showed me the architecture of exploration; the many
ways images can merge into brilliant displays of meaning;

      the many ways the silence of sound can erupt
into a thunderstorm of distinction. It was my human nature
before as a child to take it all for granted but it became
my human nature as a young adult to find the deeper fascinations
of life. I always walked alone but there were always
eyes conversing with each step my feet took; there was always
a voice following me close enough to feel the breath
of curiosity breathing heavy in the eardrums
      of my imagination. Across Mulberry Street
was always something familiar—across Mulberry Street

in the glass eyeball of a store front property was the calligraphy
and poetry of my own reflection

and I never saw it until I discovered the human nature
                                                                                   of vision.

One Moment

The trees are bare today as they reach out
into an open temperature of stillness with branches
that are waving to my eyes in a perfect salute;

      time is staring at me through a fragmented window
      just clear enough to see the energy of my mind.

Thoughts clutter in a silent rewind
as I sit here recognizing all I have come to appreciate
through loss, emptiness and the promise of renewal,

      and as the clouds massages the sky into a gentle
      relaxation, I am softly whistling the tune of faces

who have always smiled at me with warm voices;
loved ones who have gone but continue to touch my heart
with a paralyzed tenderness that never loses feeling.

      They are the brightness that has led me to healing
      all those dark, gray covered days where sadness and pain
      met on the battlegrounds of my emotional disdain,

they are the memories I embrace and hear
in times I give in to the luxuries of life's fear;
moments I hide just to observe the mysteries I feel inside.

      They are the reminders telling me that the presence
      I have become is a tribute to the appreciation
      and value of every enjoyment of vision we see

as it only takes one moment to breathe
the freshness of connection; it only takes one moment
to believe and receive the hands fate has extended

into our lives and it just takes one moment--this moment—to give gratitude
to all who have strengthened my soul

    into these awakening moments of solitude.

Poetic Rhapsody

This is the wordplay of my heart
dancing on a thunderstorm of emotion;
      raindrops drizzling a haze
inside the sensory zone of an inspirational maze;
      a duality in devotion.

I am the photographer capturing the flaws
      of perfection as all that is brilliance
becomes the magnification of the human laws
within the hands of nature's resilience.
      I capture it all; the strangeness of the sky
puffing on a sunlit cigar exhaling clouds
that blanket black birds
      that fly in the formation of a metaphor
with no true analogy.

It's all open to the interpreter who admires
and conspires to find the hidden truth
under my own fingertips
      as I am the magician turning tricks
with stanzas without losing…meaning.

I am the lover caught in the passion
      of literary execution triggering feelings
from what is ordinary in everything around me
      into explosions of the extraordinary

as my vision is the windowsill
      of expression;
literary phrases dripping from an ink
that is inspired
      through the love of poetry.

Something Said The Wind

The day was a golden smile as my mind sunbathed
underneath the gaze of the tender skies
as shades of blue eavesdropped through the clouds
of blanketed eyes. I sat in moistened sand
looking out into the distance/a distance
cluttered by the fascination of time. There was nothing
but me and nature gathered on this textured land;
a land of escape and a place that pleasured my thoughts
and tickled the sensitivity of my admiration.
I was alone as the air dimmed into an azure fragrance
of dusk decorating my vision with a dark orangey
kind of blue as the ocean waves massaged my footprints
into the perfect sequence of relaxation.
My journey was a stillness steadily drifting
with a slight breeze that whistled nature's music;
a soft sound of enrichment that made my heart dance
and remember the dreams of my soul.
It was always my goal just to be; just to exist
in moments of serenity allowing myself to listen
to what life was whispering through the air
and that day became a portrait of clarity
as the wind blew into my pain the many measures
of healing—a same wind that answered my reluctance
of all that was revealing. Something said the wind
that day; something told me to survive.

It Came To Me In A Dream

I stood here before; *right here*
in the center of a moment watching my own existence
romance the skies of time with elegant
touches of prismatic duration.

      But these were not my hands;

these were the hands of history
massaging everything that is *now*
into the relaxation of reoccurrence;

      of momentary fingerprints smudged
down the glass of fossil images reflecting
faces emerged within visions of sound/silent
but heard brightly in mutation.

      But these were not my ears;

these were the ears of sight
listening once again to the sweet melody
of imagination as it walks
on hard wood of oak waxed by reality.

I stood here before; *right here* again
in the middle of my mind watching jumbled
thoughts perform on the stage of consciousness

      with no beginning act and no ending
applause; just the stage fright of symbolic distortions
serenading with gestures of definition/undefined

but present in the clarity of sleep.

And it all came to me in a dream
that I stood here before(*not as me)*
but as fragments of imagination's reality.

Often

I lay awake/often dreaming with open eyes
about life and the study of humanity as we play house
in a society of deeds and greed habituating a world
full of translational needs and I often wonder
if I will ever capture the full knowledge of it all.
There are times I wander wondering if blind eyes
are ready and able to make eye contact with my heart
and I listen for the downpour of footprints scurrying
to be recognized by mindless drifters waiting to expose
tired souls to the different nuances of living. Often
I am just a spectator whistling with my mind
while they dance to the sound of fate taking them
and becoming them as they fall into an alcoholism—
drunkards addicted to the prohibition of life/barely
walking in straight lines and slurring their own names.
There are days I am them and often I welcome
the hangover because we breathe to change this world.
We study the air to witness new discoveries and often we
challenge the realities that make life an everyday
sacrifice of imagination. Often I stand asleep/often thinking
with closed eyes about these open walls of existence
ready to dream the next tomorrow.

Dreaming With Open Eyes

I watched tree branches dance
        to the windy blues of summer night;
heard the deep thunder of oncoming trains
rattle and shake
foundations fast asleep in the anticipation
            of midnight's hour.

And just once
 I had it all figured out as I roamed
beneath city lights glimmering
         upon the silent darkness of existence –

life was a creation of many beings
working shifts and sometimes overtime
to build the playground structured
         into our world;

Alone (all by myself) with no soul awake but me,
I admired the twinkling stars
staring down into my eyes
speaking to me in the language of humanity;

I was able to feel the heated breath
of *my* own importance
and *my* role on this cemented land of evolution.

For once, just once, I was seeing the beauty
 in all things created in destruction; –
works of art hidden on the surface
of abandoned buildings and trash covered
street corners;

graffiti painted in pretty colors translating
        the work of creativity
and discovery of growth and development.

I uncovered the reasons of struggle and success
and why all that matters matter.
Just once I figured out the puzzle of life
upon dreaming with open eyes.

Wind Chimes

        It is a s h a t t e r e d silence
that massages the eardrums
        of my mind as I dream
within the currency of timeless winds; *priceless*
arrangements of sound whistling
        and ringing in harmony
like a choir of voices illuminating in the ministry
of song.

And I am captured inside radiating
        echoes of lyrical imagery; an escape
within an escape of dancing rhymes floating
in a mist of crystallized mystique;
        soft notes of music
unique… to the naked eye
                of modulation.

These are the wind chimes of living
        that reminds me that I am alive
with their sudden motion
of delight that rattles the stillness
of the night releasing a magic
        of disappearing emptiness
inhaled through the imagination of musical
vibrations awakening
        the tone of freedom.

Footprint Of Discovery

Sand glistens between the toes
of my conscious awaking as wind clouds burst
into a tranquil breathing against the median
of my geometric being.

        I am centered

as I float without motion into the sea
of transition welcoming thunderous waves that tickle
my anxiety back to the shore of calmness

    where,

my external mind escapes
      into the internal solace

of my being.

      I am a footprint *of discovery.*

Thoughts Swirling With The Wind

Every which way the wind blows is my minds transition
into new directions of thought
and as I stand inhaling the organized confusion
of nature, I breathe in the tranquil air
in recognition of the radiance of earth's fusion.

These trees waltz as their branches
massage the echoes of my sight.
They are history, they are the shifts in generations,
they are marvelous and I want to know them.
I want to feel the heartbeat of their existence
and relish in the pulse of their soiled
tomorrow.

They are my companions as are these birds,
who sing to the notes of my ideas;
blue birds, cardinals, orioles flying in formation
as a rainbow of flight.
They are my admirers as I am theirs;
they seek to stand as I am
and I desire to fly with wings
soaring with the same beauty.

And the water is a river that sparkles
a clear story filled life. Movement colliding
with stand stills that rise in motion
but never overflows into commotion.
Chaos never swims in a river, it never gets too deep
to drown smiles.

I am here and these surroundings prove I exist;
the clouds above are whistling as the sun breaks through;

the flowers around my feet are proposing marriage
to the weeds and I hear mother nature
sitting silently with a pen in her hand writing
another chapter.
I wonder if this is all an accident she's taking credit for
or is it just my thoughts swirling with the wind.

Nauset Beach

White sand glistens against the shadows
of sunset; an orangey pink gaze smothers
perfectly lop-sided clouds that stick together
like slightly melted marshmallows
sweating from the descending blaze
of the sun

the ocean is a spectator
to my amazement as I stand here
ankle deep in the craws of sand
that warms my footprints with a soft wetness.
My mind is buzzed from hard shots
of tranquility's wind; a wind
that is whispering a kiss against my face

and here the waves are laughing at me
as I jump back from their gentle punch.
I am a virgin to their penetration
of forceful splashes

    I bet they know that

A surfer is knocked off his board.
He disappears, now reappears
and waits for another round
against the champion

       of earth's battleground

Silence is echoing (at least I think)

Or is this just the call of Cape Cod's
welcome to a familiar stranger

I am that stranger for the first time

three beers and I'm feeling pretty
damn good. But it is not the beers that intoxicate me.

It is this moment, this time, this beauty.

The surfer flips over again and here comes
the waves playing tag with my feet
as I am skipping back.

The ocean sprinkles me with a smile
as I am looking out at its forever-ness;
a live portrait still in creation.

A golden retriever runs past me…

he is chasing a ball but gives up
and now is running back empty handed

well…(mouthed)

I've only been here (for the first time)
ten minutes and so much life has happened,
so much poetry and so much history.

I like it here…so hard to leave.

So hard to sing a goodbye to this beach,

Nauset Beach.

There Again...

 The gorgeous/golden/glisten of silence
awakens as a familiar sunrise parachutes
 through the open skies of a new horizon.

  A calm/comforting wind shifts
the hazelnut sands(just barely)
as my mind once again sunbaths
under the currents of ultraviolet rays
that reach through mirrored clouds

  that reflect the deep blue
of the ocean's hue. And I am there again
inside the peaceful serenity of time
basking under a filtered air of steady warmth.

And the aroma of the sea deep massages
the shore with strong waves
  of its hands as seagulls dance
on finely sculpted pieces of earth.

I am there again
  as a voyeur to the victory of escape
watching seashells whistle their unique beauty
and drunken seals wobble with grace
nodding their silk heads with a laughter
  of happiness.

I take it all in as I am there again
with my smile as an ornament
on this picture perfect landscape
  of relaxation; a place I go

every time I close my eyes.

To Spring

It is your fragrance that revives nature's zombies
as wilted flowers smile again
and bare trees breathe
 through newly birthed leaves:

hands of chlorophyll waving to the beat
of humming birds and buzzing bees

making love to rosebuds
sprouting from soiled renewal.

It is your daylight that refuses to surrender
to time's lapsing splendor
 as I watch the freshness of your air
purify the day's journey
into a season's rehabilitation.

Your sky is clear.

To The Bird Who Sings The Morning Song

I admire the annoyance of your morning song
as you watch me through the window
of my own eyes.

      Your whistle awakens the sun
and penetrates the misty air of a new horizon.
Today you are a Blue jay camouflaging
your deep shades of many blue

against the reflection of admiration
as your radiance echoes on a bare tree branch
just out of the reach of my clarity.

      And you are the rarity
that eavesdrop on my envy as today
you will be the beauty in the sky soaring
through the imagination of human eyes

      and your wings will dance through the dancehalls
of the wind as you glide and collide
with the daily acts of living.

You are the escape free to roam
the atmosphere with your own power
and waken many dreams on mornings like these.

And you are my smile as you
nectar my soul into a blossom of enhancement.
With just these minutes of a moment
your morning song sings to me
      the lyrics of life's enchantment.

To The Tree That Once Stood Strong

Absence marks the beauty of something wonderful
and you are no longer there
sneezing against the nose of my window
with your thick branches massaging the air
        with deep tissue strokes of magnificence.

And your leaves (those many hands tickling
        my every breathe)
no longer tickle the brick stone building
that supported their playtime.
You are gone now but I still remember
how you studied me through my window
        watching my every observance
and being a witness to every tear
        and every fear as you listened silently;
sometimes I think you were the only form of existence
        that cared.

Our friendship lasted eight years
        and through that you never changed
(despite the beating from the wind/nature's
domestic violence) you were always loyal;
always there protecting me from the voyeurism
of the skies sunlight that always threatened
        to peek in
on our bond.

But you are gone now. Your strength held
you so sturdy. The thick skin of your bark
        had no fear but you couldn't take
that last forceful slap from the wind
and now you lay on the ground with roots
        up/ended and broken limbs scattered
beyond orthopedic repair.

Now they all walk by and stare at you
as you are in your peace.
Hundreds of years of visibility and only
now are you admired as you have always
been to me.

You were the best tree a man could have
and your spirit will always be there
peeking through the window
               of my life.

Florentine Gardens

A rotary of laugher surrounds the smile
of the Victorian structure standing tall on the corner
of Florentine Gardens.

Its eight front eyes gaze off into yesterday's sunset
with reflections of memories of a now empty home
      filled with hysteria but also shielded with tears

that built the foundation it now stands
      throughout the years.
And its chimney breathes a liquid existence
that rains down upon the streets; such a beautiful sound
of all the nostalgia it's presence surrounds.

A house born in 1923 birthed by the architecture
      of human hands

is more than just an old home
      it is a monument of togetherness
and the precious style of the richness
that is love. Its tiles are a faded white and unveils
some of the naked wood
      that has lasted decades of wear and tear:

a definition of durability and strength.

And the bushes protect its prize as joined hands
decorate the circular mouth; a maze of marbled stairs
leading to the open welcome of a new friend.

This house awaits a new fragrance of life
      to bind with the aroma of past perfumes
and give off that scented dialogue of occupancy.

So it stands on the corner of Florentine Gardens
whistling a historic delight as it waves to passerby's

and admirers; lurkers and contractors

with a stamped signature that says:

    For Sale.

II The Long Everlasting

"I was there, alive, amongst the magic
of existence singing along with the songs
created by time"

<u>Metaphors</u>

All around me are distractions and attractions.

The world can be a fucked up place to be, but do I pay attention more because I'm a writer? As I look out the window I see the moon shining like the glow of a halogen lamp as it stands alone surrounded by stars that sparkle like the glitter on a Michael Jackson jacket. It's natural to see beyond the curtains of my reality out a window that connects me to the simple pleasures of the eye.

Wait…let me write that down

So they say life can be a bitch or is a bitch depending on where you're at in life. I think it's more of a stage where we perform until the curtain falls. We exists to encounter problems, we glow to encounter new problems that help us either fall or rise again depending on how much strength we gained from the previous problem. And then there are those damn metaphors. Those comparisons that give us a clearer glimpse into what something is like or about.

The other day I was as cold as ice.

My heart that is (as I was angry at a few situations that caused me to shut myself off towards emotions). Being cold as ice could've meant temperature but now that I told you it was a coldness involving the emotion of anger, you know how fucking mad I really was. Sylvia Plath loved metaphors as many poets and writers do. They help the transition of our ideas and gives purpose to our description of aspects of life such as *those problems and life being a bitch.* I personally do enjoy the usage of metaphors because I see them daily even when simply looking out my window. I see them driving, conversing in crowds, jogging through parks, barking at strangers walking past and sitting on park benches. They are all around me and as a writer of poetry I just inhale their presence.

M E T A P H O R S are the distractions and attractions
that inspire.

To An Empty Chair

Here we sit alone. As
        across the room you stare at me.

I return your glance

by watching

each smile that once occupied your embrace;
        each tear that once observed your space
        and I know you can see each moment playing

the open screen of my face.

A young man once needed your frame
        and you were there as his support; a sturdy
        foundation that held the weight of his world

as he struggled to rest.

You kept him company in many times of need
as you do now. Many lives have faded
from his life but you continue to be there

as the connection to the many images
        that fragment his soul, my soul.

An empty chair;

finely placed in the corner of this dark room
        listening to my thoughts and allowing
        my emotions to once again rest on the four legs

of your shoulder.

So much more than an object

you breathe
you listen,
                and you hold me in times

I tire of standing on the hardwood floors of life.

Nothing/ness

I sat on someone else's porch one night
thinking about everything but nothing in particular.
My friend was silent(it was his porch) probably
waiting for me to leave but he was being polite
because he knew never to interrupt a poet (that's me)
while thinking. A dog barked loudly
abusing the night air with a ruckus that caused
the Siamese house cat to stutter a string of *meows*
through the screen window.
Everything became frantic at that point.
There was the conversation of noise
between the dog and the cat, neither one
seeing the other except through the reflection
of their echoes. My friend (in his 40's) decided to dance
in his own reminisce to downloaded
eighties music turned up just enough
to drown out the barking and meowing
and the loudness of my thinking.
I realized that night that everything around me
is an interpretation. The stars in the night sky
looked like traces of faces I once knew
before which to someone else would be just
a sky of constellations unnamed.
(I wished that damn dog was tamed).
And even people are interpretations; distorted
perceptions of who we need them to be
to be able to adjust to the act of introduction.
I guess the way I was thinking that night
is the way the mind functions
when there is nothing going on
except nothing which is really something
in the mind of an interpreter (otherwise known
as a poet). And I wonder how would I live

without those moments deciphered
by my own thoughts and words; how would I
write about the fragments of that moment
without recognizing the importance
of nothing/ness in this world where everything
has a reason.

A Place I Used To Call Home

This poem is a memory--
this poem is about/a place I use to call my home;
a place where this new silence I see was once the laughter
of hope and pride. A place where my young feet
use to run in the freedom winds of innocence
        but now as I look down this narrow street.
I do not recognize the sorrow/ there is emptiness
        as the price of destruction has diminished once proud
eyes and now there is no sun that rises about this sky
        just clouds that have dampened a tough cement
        into a muddy paradox of nothingness.

I use to run up and down this paved road singing
        the sweet tunes of whistled happiness
manipulating older ears into their own sweet remembrance
of how their time here use to be. The older folk
always renewed history in telling the stories of their younger years
        and now my own proud tears
bring this street back alive.

        These lampposts have lifted their rust and fresh lights
shine down upon the feet of bicycles ready to smile again
        and faded graffiti walls have washed themselves
of decay and now reach out to embrace
        trees that have lost their names; these same trees
have found their identities again and now sparkle
in the sunlight of those golden days before crime
kidnapped the aspirations of many dreams;
before poverty took over the stage of hope
and before time took away the history
        of a neighborhood that once held hands
upon this street of unity.

This poem is a memory--
this poem is about /a place that will never be again;
that place I used to call my home but my feet
still cry for this street because my heart
      has never abandoned the beauty that nurtured
my growth; the beauty once absorbed by the foundation
      of these sidewalks now dismantled
by the migration of everything that made life here
      possible...

The Long Everlasting

I walked for miles studying the golden bricks
of a dream; a road that whispered
in a glimmering brilliance in the ears
of my fascination.

My eyes listened to the heartbeats of silence
as graphically designed lamp posts
danced to the liquid transition
of stars smiling with twinkling lips.

I was there, alive, amongst the magic
of existence singing along with the songs
created by time: glamorous voices ticking
within every capture of movement.

And I walked for miles inhaling
the magical notes of a sparkling air
that never lapsed.
 I was there, alive, amongst the dreamers
of the long everlasting escape
from reality.

<u>Coffee Shop Flyers</u>

I think I'll have a caramel toffee mocha.

      "tall, Grande, or venti?"

I could tell she's been working at Starbucks
      for a while. A fake shine of happiness
on a Saturday morning with a line of customers
already with their minds made up just waiting…just waiting
      for a workaholic poet to make up his mind.

The choices in size always perplexed me. Tall is really small,
      Grande is actually not that large at all
and Venti is the classic twenty ounces of caffeine
      we crave on days like this. As I looked at the shadows
behind me exploding with impatience
      I knew what I wanted the whole time,
I just wanted to prolong the wait of predictable
      fate.

      I'll go with the Venti.

And what I mean by the fate line is that we expose
ourselves daily to opportunities of change
      with life being all about the situations
uncontrolled by the nuances of time management.
      My extra minutes of decision was changing
the pace of someone's path. Okay maybe too much
      thinking here or an excuse for not having my mind
made up before ordering.

Not that they give you much time
      to decide. But like the 'sighs' and rolled eyes
of impatience behind me, I was supposed
      to know what I wanted.

"Here's your change sir"

I was feeling lucky so I threw the two dimes
and four pennies in the little tip cup and waited
by the bulletin board pretending to be interested
      in the flyers perfectly placed in a mess
for the eyes to weed through or did I mean 'read'?.

Hot Body Contest

It took a minute for my thoughts to congest/
      the idea of people even judging other people
on something that depends on the perception of the eye.
The winner is always the person exhibiting the most "I".

Annual Art Festival On Mattoon Street

But then again it's always great when people
      have a place to showcase the talent of the mind.
And as this poster reached for my attention,
I was reminded of my own fate as I had my own
      artistry to relate. Then again who would really
be interested in thoughtful poetry?

      "Venti caramel toffee mocha!"

It's been awhile since I had a nice photograph taken of me.
      A small card on the corner of the board
made me reach and move over the AIDS walk poster
just a bit. And I wasn't ignoring the content and value
of the poster, I just wanted to get the name of the photographer;
      a name that escaped me as soon as I heard

      "Venti caramel toffee mocha".

If I wasn't so distracted by the coffee shop flyers
    maybe I would've heard it the first time.

    Oh sorry!

Shit. I felt like such an annoyance.
    But hey, such is fate.

Nostalgia

is all around me. It is in the air that laughs the smile of angels;
the echoing trees that stand as moonlit shadows
 in the eye drop of sunlight. It is the footprint of yesterday's aroma
that sits quietly in front of me on the curb of memories. Today
I am their presence; I am the childhood of ancestors who once
gave birth to the moments that now camouflage these bricks
that are now playing the supporting role on this stage of an old
neighborhood renewed. Today I dance in a pleasant silence with
each soul who wrote a chapter in my life; each unrecognized
poet who scribbled their importance in the scrapbook of my mind.
I am their brilliance as they are my design of life/this life
that has taught me loss; this life that has taught me how to breathe
a moment and sip the significance of the small things we look past
and now I can stand here shaking hands with a warm wind
blowing down from the clouds and embrace every good bye
as a new beginning and as a victory within every nostalgic touch
of history's genius.

What Happened In Harlem

I woke up one time in the 1920's. A slight drool
tickled my chin as it dripped down on the current edition
of "The Crisis". I was a long way from home and along way
from my time as I sat at a small table off to the side

       in a little Blues Café on 135th Street in Negro Harlem.
I thought it was all just a dream but the breeze of Jazzy notes
making love to my ears brought me very alive. I couldn't believe
my eyes
as on the walls were fancy paintings of the richest kind
of African art and surrounding me was the laughter

       of faces just like mine. Some darker, some lighter,
some beautiful and smooth and some rugged but defined.
A young gentleman around my age tapped me on the shoulder
       offering me a cigar. I politely declined
because I had a different kind of smoke on my mind;
the kind of smoke I was inhaling was a migration of some of the finest
       artistic expressionists in history from the south to this place
that I woke up a part of.
       A sultry voice danced its way from a small stage;
A woman of heavenly eyes and a graceful tune
massaged the atmosphere with the soft fingertips
       of her vocal chords. Bessie Smith was a woman
my grandmother idolized, and there I sat
       mesmerized
              in this escape into the nostalgia of a movement.

The man behind me was soon joined
       by a group of gentlemen in fancy suits
with smiles tap dancing through the dimmed lights
as the shadows of day turned to night. They were poets
because their words were lyrical and the admiration they had

towards each other rhymed in a delightful flow.
    I turned around to see the pages of their faces;
Arna Botemps, Claude McCay, Countee Cullen,
    James Weldon Johnson and a little known poet
named Langston Hughes. They jived about the news,
about the War, about the depression and about the way
    the female poets were establishing their own expression.

I lost myself in the moment while realizing I was there with them
    inside the fascination of a time defined.
It was a time where the negro became beautifully Black;
A time where the ghosts of slavery became the freedom
    of self-value; a time "Black" face became no longer a mask,
but a distinguished pride in the souls of these artists. It was a time
    that highlighted creativity--

    and I was there.
I woke up in 2011. A smooth morning sunlight
    drooling warmly against my face. I wasn't in Harlem anymore
but their faces were still written in my thoughts. Their words
inspired and influenced the soul of my muse.

    I was still there,

because what happened in Harlem
    has brought out the beauty of my mind.

A Simple Ginsberg

She brought it to me
      just the way I liked it.

There was nothing like a nice cold green tea
with just the right sip of ginseng. The waitress smiled
as I thanked her for remembering my style
and finally she walked to the other side of the café
where a young couple stubbornly flipped their menus
to order the toast and runny eggs with
slightly burned home fries and decaffeinated coffee.

They were not from town. A slow song
played in the background but I don't remember
the words, just a voice humming
behind me. But my mind refused to turn around
as I heard a scent of marijuana in his tone.
He sounded like one of those beat poets
who challenged academia. Again I refused to acknowledge
his presence. This was my time, my Saturday morning
in this peaceful little dump that overlooked suburbia;
      my escape from the judgment of sinners
marked with hidden tattoos of homophobia.

This was my time to examine the thoughts
of the useless and the arrogance of my own self-reflection.
The man behind me whistled annoying
the young couple from out of town who were
now on their second cup of decaffeinated bullshit.
They looked at me as if I put the dollar in the jukebox
stubbornness. The waitress sat outside on a broken bench
puffing hurriedly on a Marlboro cigarette
      with her apron blowing in an uneasy wind
that continued to blow out the lighter
just in time for her to light her second lung filler.

She was a woman with no story blowing her history
out into the air for nosey eyes to inhale. Just a witness
in this democracy of free ignorance and closed expression.
    And she exhaled
               just the way they liked it.

A bulletin board just under the Van Gogh
was filled with coffee shop flyers and business cards
selling individuality and odd commodities
that only tree huggers and retired teachers find interesting.
Maybe I was being too harsh on my surroundings
this day but the endless whistling and humming of the asshole
behind me made my mind snarl. I turned around finally
and his appearance howl(ed). His tinted glasses, his rugged
goatee and balding head resembled someone I met back
in college on the seventh floor of a library
on a dusty shelf right next to the window that overlooked
the university.

He stopped his whistling as I studied him. The young couple
asked for their bill and the waitress stumbled in
working even less hard for her non-tip (from them).
My green tea was now a glass of melted ice cubes
as I continued to research this man's structure. He barely glanced
back at me and continued scribbling in his notebook.
His pleasure that day seemed to be his lemonade
and the joy of annoying society with truth.

I turned back around just to hear him ask:
"young man have you ever been to a supermarket
in California?"

I hesitated my answer as I turned around. But he was gone.
He was who I thought he was

and he challenged my critique
just the way I liked it
on a simple Saturday, sitting in a simple café
with a simple Ginsberg.

This Side Of Bukowski

I think I saw Bukowski sitting on the edge of an old
rustic porch right in the deep smile of Block Island.
      The night's breeze glimmered over his never ending forehead
and I could smell him in the whisky of the air. His shadow
wore a gray peppered hair and a rugged beard
that blended in with the smoky haze of humid fog as his
breath energized my mind with an inspirational type of smog.

His cigarette dangled slightly from the side of his raspy cough
and his small frame just barely filled the straw weaved chair
that he stole away from my vision. I thought that I was crazy
and so he grinned as he sipped on a 1984 flavored
type of wine and spit it out on the curb
      because it wasn't sour enough for his liking.
"You have to die a few times before you can really live."
He muttered. And if this was his life as death
he was making the most of it by stealing my thoughts
for more than a moment.

The thing about this man named Charles is he made
the most prevalent of minds second guess their
own sanity; he made the kindest of souls reach deep down
and find that piece of mescaline that turned their
sweet hearts into a raging abstract of poetry. He didn't believe
in rules because rules were for those who wanted
to be under control in this crazy swirl of imagination
we call life.

      I never personally had an opinion of Bukowski
until then/until now/until I think I thought I saw him
in the gaze of his misery wishing the world well with an eyewink
of drunkenness. Life is one big poem full of shit
and you haven't written a good poem until you've

pissed someone off. That's what he told me anyway
and I believed him because I think I saw him
floating gently across the Atlantic
      pissing obscenities at the stars.

Off The Corner Of Main Street

Dimmed lights, a soft jazz silencing the whispers
of patrons scattered in cherry wood chairs
as the shiny, freshly polished marble floors glimmered
their shadows: decorations that flowed with the
ambiance of saxophone blares and the fragrance
of vanilla bean mocha blended
                with caramel lattes.
It was just a little café
              off the corner of Main Street.

The bitchy waitress refilled my slightly gingered green tea
as I sat by the window; the tinted window that masqueraded as
my flat screened television set turned to the channel
of reality as the mid-March stubborn wind played
patty cake against the window.

Characters scurried by
with places to be and people to see.

        I took a sip
and burned my lower lip. I stared over at the waitress
who glared back at me with eyes telling me to leave
her the hell alone.

        The service sucked ass.
But I still sat there in this little café
 off the corner of Main Street
.

I watched this woman covered in black fight
against the remnants of winter;

        hat threatening to leave her,

scarf strangling her with warmth
protected her from the frost of the busy street.
She looked lost, confused…perhaps desperate.
Then an echo drifted through the ally from between the cafe
and boarded up convenience store.

She looked back, hesitated
then hurried into the distance of lurkers and agitated
beggars. If only I could've known her story.
                 If only.
But alas, maybe it's up the interpretation of my imagination;
a timely inspiration.

A bitchy waitress who served overly hot beverages
and evil in-character stares
but there, in that café, I was served with scenery and action
that was more than enough to feed the appetite

of a poet*!*

Off the corner of Main Street,

this woman showed me a poem,
written on this half stained wrinkled napkin.

Dining In Connecticut

West Hartford was the good part of town, the part of town
 I didn't mind being noticed in. To be there meant
a certain kind of status and a different flavor of attitude.
So I played the part.

      As we stood outside experiencing the air
of Farmington Avenue I watched observers drive by
admiring the artistry in the window front of *Grants*.
It was a restaurant decorated in the appropriate attire
      mystifying an aroma that deciphered my taste bud's

desire; A place worthy of its genius in hospitality
very well worth the twenty minute wait facing a wind
      just cold enough to make my mind shiver.
The night was filled with the taste of a nice Italian wine;
very fine
      and wet with smiles and a gentle intoxication.

I started to wonder how I would fit in; a Black man
mixed in with many White faces always made me
      pay attention to treatment a little more/not that I
expected it but life taught me to be realistic.

'your table is ready'

The host was a little boy barely twelve donating
his time to the family business. To him, we were just another
party of four dining on a Saturday night.

      Inside was a nice sight. A nice décor frame working
 the walls and floors; the lights dimmed just right to see
the worth in the style of the tables.

We were seated in a booth and greeted by a waitress
who nicely smiled her name;
a name we didn't promise to remember
but should've because she remembered ours.
	I was fascinated with her polite delivery
and the way she recited the special of the day
without losing eye contact with me.
	If anything she treated me better than everyone else
at the table. She was down to earth and hiding
behind the tiredness of twelve hours on her feet.

	She gave us a moment.

The menu was an orchestra of poultry and pasta dishes
	with names I couldn't pronounce. I looked around
knowing I was going to order the burger, medium well
and covered with crumbles of blue cheese.

  It's what I craved.

I waited for eyes to stare back at me, as I looked around
at the different passions of people sharing in enjoyment.
	Each was like an appetizer with a delicious presentation.
An older couple to my right shared a filet and spoke to each other
with their eyes. So many years together and sill in love;
like two teenagers on a first date they giggled endlessly
in their own language and ahead of me was a group of guys
dressed in ties
	going over business plans and forgetting to have fun
all married to their jobs and divorced from free time.

And then there was us, four friends from different aspects
of the world sharing a moment of connection;
	laughing about dreams and discussing
common themes. We enjoyed the service and the service

enjoyed us. I fit in and it was a great reminder
>of the progression of society. Then again Connecticut
always treated me well and so did *Grants*. The experience
left me with a tip about the nuances of life.

We all struggle to fit in as we all remember to take the time
>to live like the elderly couple who grew young
and like the businessmen we can get lost in the transition
of obtaining that status that gives us the value
>we think we need; most of the time it's just all greed.

So I sat there, dining in Connecticut observing
life and being a part of the atmosphere of achievers
and nonchalant believers. I was one of them as for that night

>I played the part.

Washington Square

This is not just anywhere. This is where dreams step on the stage
               of life and this is not a show on Broadway.

        This is better.

Traffic is beatboxing as the November air is rhyming
          with a reefa scented air; a pollution that makes you feel good.
        And this isn't Hollywood.

This is better.

Eighty-one degree winds drifts in and out the mouth
       of mother nature. For this moment Fall has turned
      into a magician
         transforming Greenwich Village into tank tops and plaid shorts.

A tap dancer with a Mohawk choreographs a vision
     in the minds of his cohorts.
Their faces shine sober with his dreams
      as they sip cheap rum out of plastic 16 oz.
    Coke bottles and clap out of rhythm

      to a trumpet players symphonic wisdom.

 A photographer snaps a picture with his ears
of an Asian man is whining the blues with a black man's
vocal chords. He has a dream as he stands in front of a can
empty of dollar bills and useless pennies.

     But he is heard and listened to by two elder gentlemen
playing chess; plans of yesterday's strategies
making the next move. They have conquered dreams.

Two lesbian men stand by the gates
        whistling at a hemmed up skirt making her way
        across 5th Avenue with dread locks bouncing.

She is an inspired actress putting on a free show
for high eavesdroppers with the munchies for talent.
She hasn't found her dream. But someone else has
        as she is approached by a man with a beard
and see-through sunglasses handing her a key
        to an audition of inspired hearts.

The curtain closes.

Next scene act four has a gay man reciting poetry
to his "amour". In an Allen Ginsberg voice
he holds the hand of his lover with a kiss as they become
a free verse in front of open minded observers.

        They are the dreams of passion.

As the day fades NYU students
        argue with brilliance as pages shuffle
and eyes perform for the part of the highest degree
in gaining knowledge from everything around them.

They have created dreams our of stenciled minds
in the center of this park called Washington Square.

III. Through These Eyes Only

"The world is our playground/a creation
to explore; a place to endure,
a place to curiously fall and a place to freely soar"

Genius

    Gray wired nappy hair; skin a hesitated bronze dipped a slight edge of dirt. He had a grumpy beard that gazed out towards the oceans of a faded sky wildly swirling in the mist of dust. His hand loosely gripped a half pint of Smirnoff as his eyes mirrored a drunken sobriety and a crazy stare. There seemed to always be a position for him on life's street corner; a place he stood to preach silence to a noisy nosy world. Sixty-three years born he learned how to scare strangers just enough for them to realize the truth about his battered feet from his three decades living on outrageous streets. He captured a madness that made him inhale air in a new formation of breathing as he recognized his own genius in the face of insanity. Every now and then I would see this crazy man and I would always avoid the microcosm of his appearance because he scared the shit out of me by making me think.
    As a writer, a poet, a creator and an observer I have a similar mind. There is madness within me; a needed madness that helps me make since of this world. Although controlled I sometimes lose my mind and stand on street corners with other poets finding truths in tiny doses and inhaling interpretation as new meanings of understanding and perhaps even new reasons for translation. As poets, we preach through words what this man preaches through his eyes. We preach our journeys of madness through observance and as witnesses of many forms of darkness; darkness sometimes even disguised by light and beauty. With our inherited genius we seek what others never bother to find, we smell aromas that others may not find a scent and we feel the smoothness in what others may understand as being rough. Gray wired nappy hair; skin a hesitated bronze dripped in a slight edge of dirt describes a genius. This man I reflect has taught me to forgive sanity by embracing just a little bit of insanity. I need to think as a crazy man to understand the undertones of creation both out there in the world and within the focus of the mind.
    Bald head of smooth sand paper stubble; skin the shade of a dark caramel pleasure. I have a curious goatee that drifts off into a new consciousness. My hand tightly grips the pages with the ink

of adrenalin as my heart pumps to the steady beat of metaphoric palpations. I have written in words my own madness and I scare the shit out of that sixty-three year old genius because in the avoidance of my eyes, during those memories that I pretend to not notice him, he sees that I understand his language. The only difference between me and him is that he makes the world listen by shouting; I make the world listen through writing but the madness within us makes us both poets.

Through These Eyes Only

His mind is like an overheated engine pulled over
into the broken down lane

      of frustration

he waits and waits to be seen as he stands
at an abandoned bus stop waving to be picked up

      by observing eyes speeding by
      but they only see him
           as a crazy man.

I see him standing in the cold as angry winds
barely blemish the cruelty in his cheeks;
I am a witness watching

      but,

through these eyes only I see the deeper pain
driving out into a traffic of adversity
and he has no breaks to stop his faith
from crashing.

      I see him as a desperate man.

And walking past him is a victim of homicide
with her heart murdered by deceit;
a love now laying outlined on an adulterous curb
surrounded by the yellow tape of caution.

      The investigation has been closed.

She drowns in tears that force a smile
but her eyes are blank as she wanders
through crowds as an invisible soul.

    Her 'hello's' are barely answered

She is seen as a whisper in the sight
of on goers hurrying to forget her face
but I see her reflected through windows
that has stopped reflecting in her world.

They see her as a quiet stranger

    but,

through these eyes only I see her *his*-story
being skimmed through by the fingertips
of eyes that only read what they want to read,
but her pages expose her

    as a strong woman

I watched their connection explode
on the big screen of life; a screen
split in half by two defining moments

    of perception.

1924

He said the white man only turned white
when he was angry and I listened on
      as he spoke with the youthful voice
of an eighty-six year old Black man spirited by his life
and recognized in his wise sense of pride.

      His soul was too deep to hide. Hat slightly
tilted to the side covering one lazy eye;
      shoes freshly shined to match a dark
skin blackened by the heat of the deep south.
      His clothes matched his smile/bright,
colorful and worn to fit. He grew up a child
in Birmingham, Alabama
and studied life like there was no tomorrow.

      When he spoke all ears took a front row seat
because he was a man who defeated age/still standing
strong and tall on the grounds of a car dealership
      searching for a new companion;
      a companion he called his car because he couldn't own
a woman. That was his words
as he grinned. And we were just 'young fellas' to him
      because he saw in our hands
so much more of this world to grasp
as he has seen it all and lived through war;
he has watched the sea empty into new lands
and has breathed a sky that has parachuted
      through new technologies.

Through his heart I was inspired
      as I witnessed the aroma of generations
amongst the genetics of a soldier
who fought on the battlegrounds of free-
dom simply to be a connection

      for those of us lucky enough to be there
that day. He taught us to enjoy each moment
and embrace each set of eyes that said 'hello'
because you never know when you'll get
      the pleasure to say 'goodbye'.

and as he stood like a monument
      shining in the glory of past days,
he became a birth of genius like he was
in 1924.

One Day In 1960

The sky was some kind of blue laced with a sparkly gray
as the sun tucked its right eye just behind
the conjunction of two tall buildings that stood
        abandoned. A blood stained Brick faded
cleverly into the stoned foundations of tenements
once filled with life. Dumpsters filled with yesterday's trash
 parked themselves under musty fire escapes of a rusted
black that migrated parallel to the distance of my eyes.

My feet shuffled with a hesitant speed
deeper into this silent ally; an ally darkened by filtered
lamp posts and the outline of a figure who finally
exposed his face to the study of my imagination.
        His hands were rough with a tint of dark beige
as they clutched for warmth against his shivering body.
He had shades of silver camouflaging his beard
which highlighted the wired glasses decorating
        the frame of his nose. He wasn't homeless,
he just enjoyed being there just to prove he never left.

The slight snarl in his grin whispered to me
that he remembered being a seventeen year old immigrant
with hopes and dreams – with visions and fascinations
 awakened through the art of his inspirations.
        He grew old as a Bostonian writing the paths
of his life through echoes of time but never forgetting
        the identity he paved in the memory of this alleyway
that connected us together for a moment
            inside the intellect of modern literature
as soul mates challenging existence
with tomorrow's penmanship.

I read his words through his eyes and translated
his heart by the influence of his voice. One day in 1960
a young man discovered his art, he mastered his vision
through the technique of written word.
      He lived the American dream by discovering
the breath inhaled by believers and exhaled
      by achievers.

      I turned the pages of his ambition and found myself
there with him. His book was left there covered by a golden
glaze of dirt but I feel It was finely placed for me to find
over fifty years later proving his presence was real.
One day in 1960, on a day dampened with warmth,
I found the inspiration
      to live forever

Miss Jackee

She believed in miracles because she lived a miracle
        and in a dimmed room filled with unfamiliar faces,
        the inspiration in her heart glowed and lit up the room
as the bronze of her skin shined brightly within the ambiance
of laughter and playful chatter.

There wasn't a moment her mind didn't smile;
there wasn't a moment I didn't hear her voice
rejoicing in a soulful dialect that had everyone/around her
enthralled in her words. Her cheeks were rosebuds
blossoming into a brownish red every time her
        face laughed; a color perfectly matching
the technique of the shawl she wore-- strategically placed
around shoulders that once cried.

She was a woman wise with grandeur; a woman
my eyes told me was in her late thirties and life
placed in her fifties but the spirit of her heart
        gave off the magnificence of a woman/ageless.

As she spoke I heard within her tone the voices
        of bravery, sadness, fear, strength, defeat
        and hope. She talked about a little boy she tutored and guided/
        lost temporary on the wrong path she reached him
and turned him back into the dream he had to be
for in his self-believing he would find the structure
of achieving.

She talked and laughed about her days in the projects
and how togetherness was formed despite
not having much. Everyone knew each other's names
and held each other's hands in the times of need
        when the angers of poverty sought to be freed.

I found myself at her table finally introduced. Her soft hands
       shook mine as she asked me if I was also a teacher.
I responded with a nod that I wasn't but she stared at me
never letting go of that warm smile that was still fresh
       with tears.

It was then I recognized she lost a son too soon. The pain
guided her to the appreciation of the small things in life
we start to believe are meaningless. She talked and shared
of meeting her son's childhood hero. A man she recognized
       one day at a charity event; a man she only knew
as a football card hanging on her son's wall.

Her eyes glimmered as she told me how she believed
       the moment to be a miracle. She was given
the chance to meet someone her son worshipped
and it was a little thing like a football card/something
she always looked at as meaningless that connected her
to the aspects of her life that helped her grow
       and it was this little something meaningless
that turned into a meaningful friendship keeping
her son alive.

       I believed in miracles because she was a miracle.
She taught me that night how to live and enjoy the moment;
how to appreciate the little things and that we all are a value
       to someone even when we think we have no one.

That night I realized that I was indeed a teacher—
       and she educated me as she danced into the night
       showcasing the rhythm of all her experiences
       in a graceful pattern of life's choreography.

She was a woman, a mother, a daughter and a believer,
       her name was Miss Jackee.

Let Him Be

So I've seen him every day now for the last few months
of forever. Sitting up there on that crooked old shacked porch
rocking in his oak cherry rock chair with eighty-five year old bones
stiffened and aching but full of history and soul.
I never spoke a word to old man Chester Brown but I feel
I know him well.

Suspenders holding up pants that are too big
to fit around his arthritic worn away hips, always had an old
1965 Boston Red Sox T-shirt on stained with all his years
of experience. And that hat, boy, he always has that hat
covering his baldness and tilted to the side as a reminder
of his smooth, lady man younger years. Hell some still say
he's a lady's man. Always knowing how to use his charm
to get his way, and always orchestrating the right tone of voice
to make smiles dance.

They say he's too old to be living over there
on his own, too buried by age to be over there rocking with loneliness;
 too old to be smoking that old pipe blowing his smoke of glory
out into the air of history. They want to put him in a home
and take away his comfort ; they want to take away his raggedy
radio that only gets the AM stations that he listens to everyday;
they want to take away the half pint of whisky in his side pocket.
Yeah he takes a swig every couple hours but it makes him
feel less pain in his swollen feet/it's not hurting him so let it be.

His mind is still right and he can tell you stories as far back as
fifty years ago like it was yesterday. His body may be old and crumpled
but that old man has the spirit of a young boy tap dancing
making the sound of magic. He's not bothering a soul, if anything
he's showing us the art of living. So I say leave him alone
and let him rock in his chair to the music of his proud beating heart.
Let him be happy and restful; let him live his own way
and go when he wants to go. Just let him be…let him be.

The Young Americans

Many say they are nuances as they study
their own adolescence with rebellion.
They masquerade in front of these storefronts
        and on these busy sidewalk curbs
as challenged faces barely old enough to cry.

As I walk…

a young Asian girl stands in my way
as I try to get by. She is smoking a thin cigarette,
slightly puffing from the side of her pierced lip.
Her left hand is covered by a black glove
        as she ignores my presence
by rolling her eyes with her other hand.
The expression on her face gives me the middle finger
but the sadness in her stare
        politely asks me to notice her.

She is there quietly singing with a loud
voice in style. Misunderstood by the nature
of her appearance is a girl searching for her place
in a world ignoring her,
        telling her she's no good.

As I watch…

a skateboarder showcases his tattooed anger
        by blindly shifting out into the open street
of passing strangers. He is risking his tomorrow
and they are risking his discovery
as they honk their horns to the glare of his eyes
shouting 'fuck you'
        as he pushes his board with worn down
Sketcher sneakers.

For the moment the stage is his
       as his spiked Mohawk makes its way
to the other side of the street where a group
of Black and Latino kids battle back in fourth
in a lyrical game of rhyme.

Their words are fulfilled by their hardships
as their voices express the conflict
of human struggle. They speak the language
of adulthood from the bodies of children
hardened by the victories of poverty.

And as I listen…

I hear the breath of a generation wheezing
in the fields of definition. They are an asthma
as they seek to open new lungs in the dampened
air of expectations.

They are the young Americans -- a new age
of voices traveling through different languages
for growth
       and for the freedom *to be heard.*

Niche

They stand where no one else dares to stand;
these travelers
waiting and ready to find their role
in the secrecy of life and urgency of existence.
And their eyes are hungry for something
         to write
as they study the foundation of brick/layered
roads leading to absence.

They feel what no one else cares to feel
as they compose translations
with ink covered minds leaving stains
tracked across the brilliance known as nothingness;
     exposed
and hidden meanings of explorations deciphered
through the genius of their architecture
building literary structures of magnificence
on the land of poetic decadence.

And they express what everyone else fears to express
ready and able
to relate to the obscene and subtract
from the awareness of erogenous scenes
        something real
as they journey to find their own discovery
inside the critique of human emotion.
They wander paralyzed in time
        becoming historians of the moments,
these poets
uncovering and revealing
        their niche
like a sheltered rosebud blossoming
into the open air of something surreal.

Our Playground

Laughter always needs a place to play;
a smile molded out of tears
when sadness greets us
and we're introduced to our fears
tells us we're strong and able,
resilient and stable

The world is our playground/a creation
to explore; a place to endure,
a place to curiously fall and a place to freely soar
as we grip onto the monkey bars of life
we hold tight afraid to let go
instead of enjoying the experience
in capturing the rush of living
we sometimes give up
and fail to realize the joys
we are given.

We learn to balance even when emotions
weigh reluctantly.   Like a seesaw
we have to find the equilibrium
between negativity and positivity
as we find our growth
upon the mooch of creativity
and we swing high to rise
kissing the sky

but when the pendulum of our spirit
slows down, our excitement slowly die
but laughter always needs a place to play
because the world is our playground
where happiness
            surround.

IV. The Evidence Of Existence

"I am their perfect fear; a constant reminder
why they should care
about what my presence is and had written
on the blank pages of a judgmental society."

<u>Brilliance</u>

I couldn't pronounce genius...
    so I called her brilliance as she staggered down Forest Park Ave. She wore a heavy coat in sixty-five degree weather perhaps protecting her from the coldness of the world. No one seemed to notice her even though they couldn't help but stare but this lady didn't seem to care because in her eyes were the definition of importance as her focus was on survival. Her feet were at a high IQ level as they paved the way through hard times guiding her down paths of misery and up hills of invisibility just to be visible. And her ears were the frequency of intelligence as she could hear the flaws in those with perfect sound. She had an awareness that made her different yet admired to those with thinking minds; those including myself who sat at a red light analyzing her poetry.
    I wondered where she came from and where she was going; I wondered who she was and how she came to be. There were many stanzas traced in the aged lines of her face. They were hard to read from my distance but her stature was easy to skim and I recognized a woman written by only the hands of life. The ink that rained from the shadows of the lavender scarf she wrapped around her head was the study of world full of anguish and bad luck. As the light turned green I was able to slowly drive by but my thoughts were still at a red light thinking about her and the next person she will connect with. I even thought about the next person who will ignore her and miss out on the intellect of her presence. It can be just that easy to interpret someone we don't know just by noticing and she felt me notice which made her smile. I saw it in my rearview mirror as I looked back. This woman; this poetry with a tortured heart and unknown to existence could still smile and obtain life.

To me it was brilliance.

Empty Streets

Imagine if/images reflected through store front windows
were kidnapped by extinction;
no more homeless cries were heard
from the voice of hope
starving for just one nickel one dime
        maybe a quarter.

Imagine/ no more traffic jams
during rush hour;
no obscenities polluting the air
with frustration as restless souls drive
through streets of desperation
just trying to avoid the car wreck
of economic pressure.

Imagine/ walking down sidewalks once filled
with many colors of emotions
and now seeing invisible faces.
no eyes staring back at you;
no crowded noise filling your eardrums
with everyday words. Imagine if/ it was all taken away
and we were left with empty streets.

Battle Scars

I see the battle scars
unhealed amongst the streets
struggling to stop the bleeding
of starvation and despair
their saddened eyes stare back at me
these battle scars I see
fighting to survive the night
they are soldiers in their own right;
they are America's forgotten children
exposed on poverty's front line
conquered by evaporated hope
with dreams destroyed in life's battles
they are the Homeless seeking shelter
the frustrated begging for change
they are the battle scars I see
searching to be healed

The Evidence Of Existence

Trash filled truths cluttered along faded sidewalks
laying still in motion begging to recapture decayed
dreams from growling lampposts where hope once
        leaned;
shattered emptiness laying between claustrophobic
alleyways reaching out from the shadows of intellectual
prostitution selling the body of their thoughts
for just a piece of the evolution their life once
        gleamed;
they are the hopeless; the forgotten; the lifeless
barely standing/stumbling along curbs of emotional pain
just wishing to regain
        that one reason to exist; that one reason
to find the urgency of exposure. They have voices
that reach beyond the shadows just to seek
        through the visions their souls speak
to be heard and just for the rights to be understood
in a world where their tears have been plagiarized;
        a world where their hearts have been hypnotized
        and a world where their strength has been paralyzed
by ignorant eyes refusing to recognize their humanity
while silencing their pleads for help with arrogant profanity.
        They are the idealists, the realists and the pessimists
resurfacing to remind the optimists
that they are there and everywhere
        and going nowhere anytime soon
because the depths and solitudes of poverty
will always be here in every fascination of experience
as there will always be a hunger to progress
        even through those times of distress
but with movement we can't leave behind
those lost in the fields of regression
        as they are the evidence; they remind

us not to take the air we breathe for granted
      they prove every aspect of why we exist
in this temporary shelter of life.

The Lyrics Of Her Song

She was a whistle sitting silently in front of corner store
with her home wrapped openly around her
        exposing her life and the orchestra of her tears.
But no one seems to care
as she is stepped over and stepped past
        like an object just in the way.

Everyone seems to ignore what her eyes have to say.
I stood there at a cross walk
        in the middle of June day with sweat
dripping rapidly down the back of my mind
as I caught the song of this woman who is sometimes there
        and sometimes everywhere
but often nowhere. She had a stench that hummed
for a nice bath filled with hope
because for years she has had to cope
        with the stares and coldness
of a world that pretends she is just an excuse.

Her pride has been kicked with abuse
as the slow tempo of her voice has asked for help.
She wasn't America's favorite song
but the way she caught my attention
        there was no doubt the singing of her heart
was a vision that did belong
        as she sung to me.

She was homeless but her strength
stayed strong and in her lyrics was a woman
        who had dreams that were battered
by the fists of a mental illness that kept her
        unable to hold on to the definitions of herself.
She was hungry but her starvation

      was the neglect from the hands that failed
to reach back as she grabbed
for a recognition to be understood
      and to just be seen as a human being.

She was angry but continued to smile
      because she knew she was a song
with lyrics that could change a life
      if one just listened to the sight of her
sitting there covered in clothes that haven't been
      washed since the last time she was able to laugh
which was the last time she felt she existed.
She sung to me that day a song
      with lyrics that has become the music
in my heart

Broken High Heels

The scars still remain and hurt radiates the same
as it did that night his invasion changed the direction
of her name.

She sits on the side of a lonely curb
watching strangers walk past her as the mascara
still drips down a memory
         she wishes she could tame.

But the scent of his hands still linger
and the smirk on his face still surfaces as the reflection
of his violent game; a game that ripped the fabric
of her trust and invaded the insides her heart.

A world ripped apart;
an anger that will not depart
she is someone's mother; someone's sister;
someone's daughter seeking answers
and support to build a strength and create a voice
         that will empower others in her position
to raise up and realize their self-worth.

She is the symbol of survival, victimized
but never broken; brutalized but remaining
         outspoken.

A crowed rallies around her as she stands
with her broken high heels
even taller and stronger
         as she recognizes that she is not alone
on that curb. She is one of many harmed
by the forceful weakness of abuse.

Even though the tears still stain the pain
she has risen above
and redefined her name; moved forward
and conquered the shame
    by taking back her name.

She Use To Be That Girl

She was that young girl I used to see
        on the corner;
a daily fixture on the Boulevard
underdressed and overexposed
        to the nightlife;
an advertisement for male strangers
seeking that twenty minutes
        of unpleasant comfort.

She was that girl I used to know

        working the streets to survive
as she was living the life of a hustler
stripped of self-worth
        strolling the night
with her six inch pumps
        just to make a dime;
black mascara steadily flowing
down her face created by
tears that streamed all the time
        because the life almost killed her
the same day she recognized
        she was no longer alone.

Then she became that woman I see

sitting in the uptown deli

dressed in the finest business attire;
an unrecognizable image
        of the girl she used to be.

A woman of success, no longer an object

of temporary pleasure: ***a true treasure***
who recognized her world
        could be much more

than those harsh nights
she spent in the cold only recognized
    as a whore.

Now she is that woman looking down
at those same streets through the window
of her upscale office
    making money with her mind;
an accomplishment
    built from the strength
to redefine her worth,
an empowerment fueled
by those feelings of disgust
    in the life she once lived.

And of all that she was;
    of all the desperate nights
she spent selling her body;
of all the tears she cried
    with no hope of a future;
of all the many times
    she was seen as nothing but

        She can now hold her head

up high and be proud recognizing

    she used to be that girl.

One Man's Own

If you look close enough you could see the scent of blues
whistling through the un/inspired eyes of filtered tears
empting from a man traveling through too many years
      of mental illness;
if you stop and listen long enough you could smell
the whisper of a lost soul gasping for the breaths of help
to rescue his life,
      and
if you talk to the study of his appearance just long enough
his clothes would tell you the disappointments
and sadness he has been exposed to; a dampened rain
of pain has stained his wrinkled jacket
      and yet he refuses to cry
because he has stood in those same heelless shoes
for thirteen years watching strangers pass by him
      without a single stare.
His outgrown pants would tell you the story of a man
who was thrown out on the streets
of schizophrenia exposed to a world stepping
over his mind every time his reflection
      asks for spare change.
He is judged because his home has no doors,
chastised because his appearance lurks in alleyways
shadowed by overpopulated sidewalk curbs
      and stared at because his smile
fades on a face that once was the memory
of a father, husband and an achiever
who once was a believer
      in his own ability.
It is a song you never think you would see
until the situation stands right in front of you.
If you stop and pay attention to him
      for more than a minute

>　　　you would make his day
by showing that you care
because one man's own words is not enough
to show the history of a battle he continues to fight;
one man's own tears is not enough
to hide the anger and confusion he witnesses
>　　　inside his own heart,
and one man's own silence is not loud enough
to echo the human condition that the paths of life
leads you in its destination towards
>　　　*hope.*

The Thoughts Of Curiosity

I am just a fragment of a human object
to their minds. My scruffy beard and dirty hands
      scare them.

I wonder if they even take the time to think about
where my heart has been or the depth of every scar
surfacing my being.

Look at them over there with their fancy cars
and greedy kids giggling with ignorant eyes.

They don't see my eyes; these eyes because they
are reflections of how quickly life can turn
and they can be standing right here dressed in rags
and turn boots holding this sign for an extra buck.

I wonder if they even give a fuck
about all the shit these shoes have stepped in
      just to survive
streets that expose me to freezing temperatures
of starvation.

I wonder if they even give a thought
to all the dirt that has accumulated on these ripped
clothes barely covering the bare skin of my mind
as I decorate this perfectly cracked sidewalk
      that time has left behind.

Look at them with their masked smiles of disguise
hiding behind the riches and fortune
of the wise.

They are so blind to their own insecurities
looking at me because I am their shame;
I am their reality when too many snorts of cocaine
bankrupts their fame.

I am their perfect fear; a constant reminder
of why they should care
about what my presence is and has written
on the blank pages of a judgmental society.

I use to be one of them. I use to look down
on people like me; the trash of American negligence.
I use to spit on every beggar for chance
because I earned every conceited cent I owned
and who were they to mooch off of my success?

But I was mooching off my own stability
and took for granted that nothing can be promised
because with one turn of fate
       all abundance of bread I fed off of
turned to crumbs and poverty kicked my ass.

So I sit here deserving of every cruel
observation because I was one of them;
I was a sellout with no soul because the money
turned me into something unrecognizable;
a broke homeless thought
traveling amongst the tampered canisters
of curiosity.

Mission Hill

A bottle of cheap whisky covered by
a wrinkled brown paper bag sat in his lap
as the half paved sidewalk supported
his beaten down, drunken old body of despair.

I was just 'bout a little boy but I remember him well.
He was the scary bum on Tremont Street who
made his rest in front of that ole grocery mart
on mission hill.

And if he was just a man,
perhaps he would've been forgotten by now,
but he had recognition in his eyes
and dreams missing from his heart that were ripped
away by life.

And if he was indeed just a man,
perhaps the humming of his soul
wouldn't have been heard as his drunkenness
cried out the songs of sober memories
of back when he was just 'bout a boy
standing on that same corner with a glimmer in his eyes
and a driven desire to see brighter blue skies.

A sip of that cheap whisky eased his pain
as he laid by the curb surrounded by clutter
challenged to ask for spare change with a slurred stutter.
He remembered who he used to be;
inspired, passionate and unafraid.
He once stood tall and proud right there
where his plastered ambition laid.

He used to sing and dance
in front of that same old grocery mart on mission hill;
had everyone stopping to watch and admire
but the hardships of life snuck up upon him
and caused his talents to retire.

I always walked past him and smelled
the stench filling the air with failure's pollution
and eyes that barely glanced at me when I called him 'granddaddy'—
too drunk in shame and misery to recognize
what he did right in life.
If he was just a man,
I wouldn't have reached for his hand but still
he wanted to remain there on Mission Hill

Grandaddy's Song

A half chewed toothpick dangled slightly
      from the side of his mouth barely brushing his gray and black
porcupine beard that covered a sixty-five year old bronze
skin which sweated the memories of Old Virginia.
      His eyes were always humming that old blues
he once whistled on the street corner of his youth;
years he barely remembered as a stroke confused his mind
and paralyzed his thoughts just enough
      to stop him from crying.

He always kept a whisky colored smile
      that held his happiness from dying but droplets
of tears pouring from his once hopeful sky of dreams
dampened his soul as he became someone he barely
recognized himself; someone once strong/a man
      who raised a family and worked the fields of sacrifice
to feed his children and heal the struggle of a wife
who stood by him even when times were tough
and the streams of faith ran dry. He was a survivor
refusing to completely fade even when a marriage failed
      and all he knew became lost in a tunnel
with only a small speck of light guiding his vision.

      I watched him as he stood in that old garden
sipping on a pint of blackberry brandy. He always wore pants
that were barely held up by a stringy belt and a baseball cap
tilted straight covering a head
      that lost most its hair back when his adulthood
met its mid-thirties. His old stained tee-shirt
laid baggy against his thinned bones and fragile stance.
The perspiration of the sun beamed on his muggy
      shoes as he staggered the blues.

  Grandaddy always mumbled a song and although
we could never make out the words, we knew that when
        he was alone in his garden, humming
 and tap dancing on the soil of life that he was in his special place;
       a place inside his tired mind where he could remind
all that he has been through and unwind
with the lyrics of his heart. Grandaddy had a song
and by just watching him we could feel the dance
vibrating decades of a journey that lead
        to the birth of all of our heartbeats
and future generations to come because of the man
who stood on failure's feet
        securing a bloodline and writing a song
with just the pen of his genetics;

a song that will echo on in our remembrance
as now that he's gone, forever in our hearts
his presence shall dance.

V. Poetry For Progress

"I have dreams of queens and kings once again riding these same sidewalks on chariots designed by the sweat and tears of ancestors who have journeyed for our freedom."

<u>Diversity</u>

Life is a diversity of tears.

    We are all the same because we cry different and we are different because we have our own ways of believing. I walk the streets at night on the feet of a tired mind watching and seeking that one vision of change. I see lampposts blink in a magnitude of light exposing eyes that hope to conquer the many forms discrimination that lurk in dark alleyways and hide behind the boarded windows of crumbling dreams. It was a long time ago when I was much younger that laughter taught me to be afraid of these same distorted streets but resilience taught me to study each insult and magnify them into new forms of compliment. I am no longer afraid of this sort of darkness because in each embrace of a new stare relinquishes that fear we develop of being an image of non-acceptance. We are a diverse determination of hope because we are not who we are through birth; we are who we are because we have to dissect and sculpture the challenges of this earth.
    On these same streets I saw a homeless white man praise a rich black man and thank him for recognizing his value as a human being. They touched each other's hands as if they were brothers because they were and because somewhere before in time their roles were opposite. I saw an Asian woman kiss the smile of a Latino woman as they stood on the same curb; one on her way home from night class and the other singing into the night with a voice heard by an elderly gay man who never thought he would see the day that a young straight man would stop to offer him a hand to help his old youthful bones a guide across a street where different cars honked out of tune towards the same opposite direction. There was harmony as the many songs became of chorus of growth and exposure. In each flaw was an originality of prosperity and I begin to feel the tears rain from a clear night sky. These were tears of joy, anguish, failure, achievement and realization; these were tears of Black men and women who challenged prejudice with pride and self-beauty; these were tears of the Irish overcoming

struggle through hard work and self-preservation; these were tears of Japanese children who were led to believe they didn't have a place in a country built on freedom; these were the tears of Jewish boys and girls born in concentration camps before they even had the chance to breathe equality and these were the tears of Cuban travelers swimming miles to rest on the land of liberty. Each of us no matter the skin we are born in have face and will challenge adversity so why not do it together in the fields where all tears have created a beautiful garden of victory.

Diversity is the many bloodlines of life.

2:26 A.M

2:20 A.M - A Saturday night has eased into filters of an early Sunday morning
and there is no peace out there. Silence has become the steady
vibrations of sirens traveling through pathways of crime. Someone has
lost a life as others stand alone in crowds searching for life.
The shades have gone down but these streets are crying
       and it doesn't even feel like we are trying
            to reach out with our eyes and wake up/we stay blind
hoping the next tragedy doesn't affect our own but somewhere
out there a mother is awakened by the shouts of a phone
as she realizes one of her worst fears has triggered never ending tears.

We sleep through the gun shots fired at empty hearts/youth
taught not to care as we hear their cries through polluted air.
We sleep through another future murdered on the stairs
of lost hope and another addiction overdosed on homeless dope.
We sleep through once recognized faces masquerading as shadows
selling their souls to strangers for a quick fix of emotional need.
We sleep through the pleading for help and the arithmetic of the numbers
growing forcing us to wake up to the living nightmare of this reality

2:26 A.M - A Sunday morning has risen and somewhere out there
lives have changed and dreams have been lost. Somewhere out there
the shades will stay down and daylight will be paused
until we all decide to open our eyes and see that we can
be the hand because it only takes six minutes to hear all the problems
and just one moment to save a life.

A City Of Dreams

He travels towards destinations of hope as the ghetto morning
smiles down on the streets that birthed his strength; the same
inner city streets he has watched deteriorate
in a loud destructive silence. Young/Black/seventeen years of age
he rides on a bus that travels through boulevards
of crime and avenues of poverty so he closes his eyes
to a new surrounding; a new place to call home—a place
where low income housing is built on the foundation of sacrifice;
a community rising in the hands of economic stability.
With his eyes closed he visions a place where ability
is the proven gift of self-awareness. He sees drug dealers
transform from narcotic pushers to sellers of independent
      thought feeding a new addiction of intellectualism;

he sees young teenage mothers grow into woman
who give birth to the knowledge of their own mind, pushing
from their womb the expression of individuality and finesse;
he sees the faces of hunger turn into faces of success
as they find the nourishment to feed the energies of natural
      intelligence. And with his eyes closed he stands as a witness
to the surroundings of brilliance. The echoes of gun shots in the dark
hours of daylight has faded;
 the aroma of police sirens decorating the night air
with brutality has faded;
the shouts of tears from the price of fear
has faded and around him only the celebrations
of victory are demonstrated.

      He smiles before opening his eyes to the harsh
reality of his world. Young/Black/seventeen years of age,
he is where the change begins—he has to become the leader
towards a new tomorrow by continuing today's journey
because in his eyes is the genetics of a hero; in his heart

is the definition of a genius; in his mind is the progression
of thought and in his dreams is hope that one day
    he will lead in this new city of dreams
and not just see it…
        when he closes his eyes.

Every City Has A Ghetto

Black top sidewalks with faded blood stains of dreams passed;
worn down cascaded buildings of abandoned hope
barely standing on foundations where tears flow – and there a young
boy stands alone with nowhere to go. His silence studies
the chaotic traffic around him as he watches
          poverty hold captive the many shades of desperation
        starving to breathe a chance to survive. Barely
twelve years old and he already knows the rhyme of death
by heart, he has watched his older brother gunned down by failure
and listened to his own mother overdose on frustration,

but somewhere, somehow he has found the motivation
to grow despite raggedy shoes holding him down
in a concrete jungle where his name is just another number;
    a statistic of the next casualty in life's drive by
    he dodges bullets with his head held high striving
to become his own definition of a survivor and an achiever
because he knows that under the same darkened sky he is not alone,
that somewhere in another city there is a **possibility** standing
silently sharing his vision of a tomorrow where

        hunger has gone extinct and no longer
crumbles intelligent minds into victims of humbled crimes;
a journey that travels reachable destinations
on the wheels of equal education and a vision promising
a victory of strength as he shatters defeat
    and stands tall on battle tested feet.

He knows he is just one of millions born into a world
with no head start surviving just to struggle and struggling
just to live. He stands alone crying a smile and encompassing
the aroma of bottled up failure because every city has a ghetto

and every dream has hope
    as this has become his inspiration
                    to believe.

Of Life's Complexity

Inspired by The Poetry Of Tupac Shakur

Those who accept simplicity
have never walked on the same side
of the street as me.
They've never watched grown folks cry
when hopes and dreams slowly die.

They've never seen single mothers struggle
or heard their cries
around dinner time
when food is scarce and not enough
to feed hungry eyes.

They've never heard the knocks of homelessness
from those working two jobs
just to survive;
beaten down by life's hardships,
no longer able to strive.

They've never felt poverty's wrath
scattered through neglected streets
where tomorrow's children play
with no funded playgrounds
and empty promises that end all feats

and they've never had to make strides
and leap over adversity
or come face to face with challenge
because those who accept simplicity
have not had to see life's complexity.

Dangerfield

There used to be so much life and beauty
on these streets even on streets that weren't beautiful
in appearance had a beauty that reflected the soul
of community.

There was a time I played on these streets
        as a child

 exploring innocence and was allowed to grow
into the environment and not away from it.

So tell me how it all changed?

When did restaurants that use to dance
along the sidewalks of Worthington street
turn into a combat zone for violence
        and random death.

When did the music end?

When did school teachers
start fearing for their own lives in classrooms
no longer designed for education
        but for survival.

When did the learning end?

When did babies start killing each other
        on the landscapes of street corners
where futures have become the captured prey
of overcrowded prisons that receive more tax funds
than the flowerbeds that rest empty
on deserted sidewalks.

When did dreams end?

When did I lose recognition
of my own city; a city that has lost its identity
within the monuments of crime
and has lost all the bare fists of local heroes;
no one is fighting back.

Guns are doing all the talking; bullets fly recklessly
over horizons once known for the foundation
of its homes. People are afraid
to be here so they rather spend their money
in other places.

So tell me

when did the beauty end?

And what has happened to the place
I was allowed to grow;

when did this become Dangerfield?

Street Corners And Hustlers

He stands
on the corner of struggle and desperation
wearing the mask of America's most
stereotyped image;
baggy jeans hanging down low,
gold decorations shining bright--
        demonstrations of glamour
        blending into the night,

but in his eyes is the sadness
of a little boy forced to be a man
        before he could grow
in the harsh surroundings of his world;
a child delivered from the womb of poverty
into an environment of failed aspirations
        and the explosion of dreams

so he stands
on the corner of fear and despair
selling poison to dependent souls
seeking a temporary vacation
from the realities of failure
        just for his own survival.

He is viewed as a thug, a drug dealer, and a threat.
But beyond the surface
is a man who has lost hope choosing to sell dope
because of the knocks of starvation
that threatens to kick down his door;
and from the sounds of homelessness
that whispers in his ears everyday he wakes.

There he stands
on the corner of destruction and crime
a representation of many but not all
who are seen as unsolvable
 in the challenging equation
                of street corners and hustlers.

Streets of Success

When they rise
      I rise
and when they cry
      I find tears in my own eyes
because like them I know
how it feels to fall and feel trapped
inside the inescapable playground
      where poverty plays

I have been there standing
in broken down streets
in the same sneakers
with the worn down soles
that have barely covered my feet.

Like them
I've leaned against the wall of struggle/
back bruised and scrapped,
tattooed scars
from the unbreakable bars
of destruction surrounding me

and like them
I thought I was too stuck
in a vortex of shattered dreams
until eyes awakened
to brighter days of possibilities--

I could turn my head
when I see echoes of me
in their face, I could forget
that I too was there where they are
fighting and clawing to find
a way out.

But I can't

because they are me
and in their hearts beat survival
        and in their eyes
are the watered pains blinking
for healing.

They are not turning to drug dealing
because they like me
want to feel that successful feeling
of simply *becoming*/rising from streets
where they had less
to the self-created streets of success

They are my little brothers,
sisters and shadows of me

so when they Rise
I too will ***RISE!***

A Poem For Progress

If wrote the best poem in the world
    I would dry the tears on the silent neglected streets
 where lampposts blink the sounds of destruction,
and in the eyes of poverty I would stare into each child's
    vision and inspire in them the hope, strength
and victory of success. I would wake up drug infested minds
who crawl the curbs of crime and instill in them
    a new rehabilitation of self-worth so they, themselves,
could end the cycle of decaying hearts.
I would touch each hand who reaches out for healing
    and warm their souls with a new feeling
                of recognition
so that they could thrive as humanitarians
and lead the way towards new paths of hope and new roads
leading the lost to revealing destinations of definition.

    And if I wrote the best poem in the world
I would allow my fingers to become the voice of dedication
as my ink tells the stories of the many lives captured and awakened
    by the reality of dreams like the little girl who
sits alone in her bedroom afraid to turn on the lights because
    the reflection staring back at her in the shadows
whisper to her that she is not good enough to be beautiful
    so she cries hides her since of self until the day
life lifts the mask off her heart and the spirit within her
becomes a new voice of beauty and pride and now she is a girl who
    walks past mirrors with her head held high
because she found the strength in self to reach her endless sky

    and through her inspiration a new fragrance of worth is
embraced
as she walks past the boy who
    sits on blood stained stairs lost in his own home.

He looks down at the scars on his legs from the abuse
of a father who is barely there--
    afraid to share his tears because the world
doesn't want to hear a young man's cry. He feels empty
but inside of him are words/many words of value
and his thoughts begin to flow out into streams of strength
    as he becomes his own man no longer unwritten
because he now fits/in this world of achievers and believers

    and yet another verse italicized in the best poem
in the world; the poem called life where progress is more than just
    an fulfilled dream.

I Have Dreams

These sidewalks crackle to the pop of tears that drop
from misty eyes just wishing all this tragedy will stop.
I look around into the silence of hearts barely beating
and recognize that hope has faded; desperate souls are bleeding.
I hold out my hand in the hope of healing
but how can I heal when I myself have scars infected
by the disappointments life has carved
into the bandages of my own believing. But there will not be any surrender;
there will not be any mask disguising me as a pretender

because I have dreams…I have dreams

that will heal these sores into birthmarks of pride;
I have dreams of queens and kings once again
riding these same sidewalks on chariots designed by the sweat
and tears of ancestors who have journeyed for our freedom.

I have dreams that this can once again be a kingdom
when we as people decide we can rise
 from puddles of poverty
and reach for the highest sky of achievement's sobriety.

I have dreams that every child in today's society
will be prepared to run the course of this life's marathon
with every finish line being reached without losing breath
or giving up on aspirations because there is no challenge
that can't be achieved when the mind and heart
is trained to believe.

I have dreams that will cure the endless deceiving
from political poets standing on podiums of propaganda
giving us hope with endless stanzas of recognition

of the problems that study and graduate on our city streets
but yet have the keys been turned in the ignition
to drive these diagrams of solutions.

And I have dreams that my mind will conquer hearts
and transcribe ignorance into a mediation of compassion
where hands will be joined for solace instead of divided
behind the bars of convicted malice.

I see through optimistic eyes despite the pathology of lies
destined to destroy but instead employ
an ink that will reach long into the future of today's truth
because I will always have scars tattooed
on the rough skin of my expression; an expression
that will never be punctured as long as I have dreams.

Miss Parks

No! No! I will not give up my seat on this bus
My feet hurt so there's no more left to discuss/
I've sat up many restless nights
As my people struggled for their civil rights/
My eyes have seen too much torture
Cast upon those who share my same culture/
I'm worn out and tired of being afraid
My bones ache of distraught and with that being said/
No! No! I will not give up my seat on this bus
I want to enjoy this ride just the same and thus/
You will no longer take advantage of my skin
Because in life that is the very sin/
That thou shall not cast hate on another
For we are all created equal to each other/
My old hands have felt too much defeat
On these storied barren streets/
So no I won't give up my seat on this bus
My name is Rosa Parks, and in my freedom, I solely trust.

The Roads Of Selma, 1963

Leaving footprints forever sculptured
on American soil... they Marched/they marched hand and hand
on a journey towards equality and for the right to have
their voices heard and have the image of their pride
permanently stamped within the colors
$\qquad\qquad$ of the American Flag.

They heard the bells of freedom ringing
as their feet walked in harmony/ a peaceful harmony
through the morning roads of Selma.
They marched with united voices that they shall overcome;
they marched with fearless hearts
$\qquad\qquad$ in wake of what may come--

--and what did come were bull whips
across their backs, *(not shattering their hope)*
tear gas in their eyes, *(not blinding their vision)*
billy clubs to their knees, *(not breaking their fight.)*

On they marched overcoming the barricades
of years and years of injustice to ensure that past silence
will be forever heard in future voices.

On they marched stepping past racism
and onto a new land/a land with new opportunity
and equality/a land of new found hope
and prosperity for generations to come.

And on they marched with new voices to be heard
and new freedoms achieved with footprints
that are forever imprinted in the soiled heart of American history.

The Sidewalks of Yesterday

Today, I walk the sidewalks of
yesterday's struggle;
I see the blood, sweat, desperation and courage
engrained in the cracks of cement
my feet now walk.

I hear the echo of voices
singing freedom's song,
the vibrations of frustration
crying the tears of pain
and in the windows of storefronts
I see reflections of those
who came before me, legacies left behind
and paths to follow

I walk in shoes more comfortable
than theirs,
but still my toes cringe
as injustice and discrimination
linger on street corners and alleys;
and still my feet ache
after many blocks of poverty
and destruction.

But still I walk,
proud and unafraid
because I know I have the heart
of a warrior inherited by their strength,
I have the fearless ambition
in my bloodline to trudge along
I have the genealogy of determination
as my fuel to continue the fight.

For I always see the images
of their shadows underneath
hundred year old trees
and always know their fingerprints
will always be smeared throughout
the history of my being,
I walk the sidewalks of yesterday
the concrete of today.

VI. Awakened

"I saw the best minds of my generation destroyed by madness, starving hysterical naked."
Allen Ginsberg

Therapy

I have been diagnosed with madness.

In other words I have lost my damn mind and I love it because I am the calculation of every equation known as a poet. I smell the acid of interpretation in the air; an aroma that inspires me to challenge the average thinking man through the filtered words of analytical vision. I don't see through normal eyes because the ink dripping through my blood is my every fascination and helps me shield away the cataracts of thoughtlessness. I am my own shrink walking the sidewalks non-sense with a (sense) of how existence frames the art work of delusion. People pass me by not realizing that I am the therapy they need to release those stories their own eyes try to hide but echo through their footprints as they stampede to the next destination of ambivalence.

Translation has no definite answer.

As poets we become the argument contained in questions many try to solve but can't grasp until they find their own madness. We don't have to make sense to be correct but we do have to give feeling to inspire. It is our ability to hypnotize the most stubborn of minds that makes us geniuses just above the idiots we are perceived to be through the fabrications of our living metaphors. I tried to escape my madness instead of accepting it. Charles Bukowski looked me straight in the eye and told me that I wouldn't be a great poet if I wasn't some sort of an asshole. At least I think that's how he phrased it when I was dreaming. But perhaps the therapy we seek is only found by living and writing and not from some sweaty leather couch in front of a professional who jerks off his mind through the stimulation of someone who is depressed for being normal.

Madness is the true equation of literary math. And they say it's all Algebra. I see my English degree is getting the last laugh. Oh and here's one to you Sylvia Plath.

Life is therapeutic when we create our own path.

<u>Awakened</u>

I am a pause stranded between the history
of tomorrow and the future of yesterday. Time
stands still. I walk with feet that travel nowhere.
Sidewalks end yet are paved by forever's hands.

Everyone sees me; I am invisible,
no one pays attention to my silence.

The sunlight heals my absence
with its radiant glow on already darkened skin.

My mind is stuck in traffic, moving steadily
with thoughts that sing, but out of tune.

Scattered movements.

No one sees my whispers, but they glance
to hear the footsteps of my words. They turn away.

I am left alone. Time rings and I un-pause. Awakened;
I open my eyes to a dream remembered.

S i L e N c E

I sleep wide awake. Eyes half open to reality;
half shut to dreams. I struggle with duality.

Sleep strangles my consciousness. Darkness
embraces light and I float on water that does not rise.

    Upon sunrise

I arise
    to my demise
failing to recognize
    the surprise
of my quiet eyes to this loudness in disguise.

I shout a deafening noise that ripples
through loud waters of a clear turquoise.

There are no notes in my music. No *bang*
in the slam of my door. No *splat* in the puddles
    under my feet!
No *cling*; no *clang!* But my ears speak.

I hear everything
    and listen to nothing
quite an interesting sound
    or is it the other way around?

I question my own existence
answered by life's ever present

    SiLeNcE.

Outcast

I walk this crowded street, running this maze all alone
with no one around me, I am far from home.
All I see is the soul of my own eyes; heartbeats stare
at my existence recognizing my absence, they do not care.
Alone in a crowd. There are many outlets but I stand still
hands are reaching for my voice; they are out for the kill.

I turn away because in this world I feel no connection
in this distorted reality where I'm lost through reflection.
There is nothing but silence in their breath; they choke my vision
because I do not belong; common awareness, faces in collision.
Alone in a crowd. My footprints are muted on pause
through the shadows of buildings exposing life's flaws.

I walk this crowded street alone haunting my path of recognition
everyone around me are blurred portraits of hesitation.
They are stranger who are walking through me
as I become blind through their conscience they become me
Alone in a crowd. I feel like an outcast inside someone's else's mind
the day parachutes into night in this flourish of life stuck on rewind.

On The Random Road Of Confusion

I have traveled past the escape of civilization; alone
on a road with no path/flesh distanced

  from the clutch of my bones.

Wind gusts blow through me as I walk statured
on a journey of confinement;
waltzing in time,

      jazz'd back and forth into alignment

by the courses of a mental mind
collapsed and awaiting arraignment.
Sentenced to darkness and eclipsed
by visions that stand everywhere. I see nothing.

A bird flies above in skies
tortured by chaotic claws drawing blood
        from my eyes.

I am a trampled echo reaching out
for the hands of sanity but coherence
turns its back on the shout of my grasp

      as I watch myself in a nightmare of illusion;
endless delusions

  on a random road of confusion.

10:53 P.M.

I'm staring out this window of no light
with darkness blinding my sight
the shadows of pine trees are peeking
at me from behind the old Victorian
over there on Magnolia Terrace/the one
with the half bricked chimney and collapsing roof.

The winds clap against the windows
as the screens shiver and curtains wave
                      to the night
and here I sit with my mind
                      inspired to write
but it's fucking dark in here --
                      the power is out
so excuse me if these words are not clear.

I can't see a thing around me except
silhouettes of objects dancing against
my slightly moon lit walls;
personified spectacles of illusion
given life by the delusion
of my imaginative brain activity.
I hear engines speeding by
as headlights are giving me momentary
light just long enough for me to vision
where they are going and their need
for the rush. My fingers want to write
                      it all down
but it's fucking dark in here.
                      No flashlight
and the jeans I'm wearing are feeling
                      pretty tight.

You ever think too much? Overanalyzing
the things you could give a damn about
when visualizations were clear
to the eyes and not just
                moments of the mind
when intelligence has that timely
                    need to unwind.

So I sit here wondering if there are mice
                and will they nibble
at the crumbs of peanut butter cookies
I dropped just under the
end table on the right side of the couch.
If it wasn't so fucking dark in here
I could sweep it all up
and not worry about rodents
starved for the mysteries of the night
the same way I'm starved
                for the realities of light.

All of this is just scribble on a blank
piece of Stafford lined paper
and now the power if back on;
            the lamps have popped on,
the shadows have disappeared
and the clock is blinking
                        10:53 P.M.

and my mind has gone blank.

Ashes

I walk through the conscience of my mind
                          afraid to fall in the fires of rage.
I look ahead leaving everything behind,
all memories torched, fear now encaged.

Flames ignite freezing my soul; empty thoughts
has invited the darkness, no longer am I whole.

I hear the echoes of the devil's name. Twisting
and turning I become his shadow through
the burning flame. Our laughter now becomes
one of the same. I melt in self-blame.

And as I look down into the black hole
of who I was, I see reflections reaching
up for me to be saved. But now to be known,
the faces crying are images of my own.

So I descend into the clutches of hell's kingdom
scalding all virtues, ashes I become.

The Last Tomorrow

Death awakens in eyes mirrored with life's coma. I am not afraid.
Time has taken me as the internal stenosis collapses;

      to rest I am laid.

I have lived to become the eventual escape of breath. Existence fights

the deep air of all my last might.

      Let me go. *The travel is over.*

      The journey empties

my being into the airwaves of eternity. Left behind are the fingerprints
of moments rewritten by the eraser of my soul. Memories bleed out

and turn into dust scattered over roads of new discovery.

      I am gone but present.

Afterlife captures the translation of my being. I am seeing

my own body regenerate into a resurgence of a miracle

as light shines into the tunnel of renewal.

 I am here but no longer there; there where I once walked
but now left alone buried deep in tears left dried
into concrete of a forever monument proving my name.
never forgotten; but tomorrow is gone. I am life's disguise;

      I am my own demise.

Life's Recipe.

Taste it: it loses its flavor once swallowed,
this feast of energy fulfilling times starvation;
an empty stomach growling full of hunger.

Today is a taste bud numb to the tongue;
the mouth waters with anticipating
teeth -- prepared to chew
into the endless feast of tomorrow's ingredients.

The stove sweats cold; another recipe walks
through aisles shopping for just the right hustle
to survive. The oven freezes into un-breathed
calories of growth fattening regret
into an overweight mind thinking on a treadmill
to gain knowledge.

And yesterday becomes a vomit staining the heart
with a stench living past the expiration date
of function and ability. The kitchen collides
until life is a fully cooked dinner
unattended. But age must eat to die.

Death is dessert.

The Light Of Sanity

I've escaped endless highways of time to find you.
but darkness has become your master
as the image of your soul
fades into the shadows
of a deep dark incoherence.

And *finally* I have found thee
shattered
       confused
              ashamed
                      and lost
amongst the powerless populations
of insanity,

but still I extend this hand
in hopes of becoming your awakening;
to lead you back to the light
of sanity
and bring you home to the comfort
and familiarity
within the complexity of my mind.

The Timeless

I walk towards nowhere to get somewhere
as my imagination become white walls
in the crowded hallway of emptiness. I am
the silence before the scream; the unforeseen
appearance that becomes visible through closed eyes.

I stand in the middle of blind vision
as a force of impact right before collision

A journey that collides with the past; breaking
through to the future but stuck as stillness;
a stillness conquered by shadows that hide
in the midst of the lights of time that life divides.

I am there even when I am here; floating
towards eternity reaching for all that is near
but pushed back because forever equals fear.

And whereas closed doorways give way to openness
moments turn into captured escape
 as I travel amongst the timeless.

Street of Consequences

Again and again I find myself standing
contemplating with self-reflective images
swirling around like a windmill stuck in time
internally roaring as a hot wind
that is fiercely blows against my face causing
electric chills that rattle my bones
and there is no one else around…

but me

and it was my choices that put me there
standing on a one way street
with no option of turning back;
a place in my mind
where I ponder all bad decisions
and indecisions, find new directions
somewhere hidden on the map of indirections
on roads I travel but often halt
speeding to a destination of my own fault.

So when I come to the corner of *"if's"*
do I turn or do I yield?
or do I continue to just stand
against new winds
The answer is found in the recognition
of the cause and effect of my own being
whereas challenge is found in the mistakes
and victory is determined by my own fate
I will fail to travel
until I look both ways before crossing
the street of consequences.

People

I see the secrets in their eyes; all of them
 as they float through earth
hidden between whispers of decency
that collide with revelations of what's beneath
their porcelain masks.

They walk delicately to avoid
cracks in the façade knowing one rumble
from the hidden
can shatter their secrecy
causing well-kept images to c r u m b l e.

neighbors seldom speak as they peek
through the tinted darkness of divulgence.
They are afraid
to be seen beyond the definition
of neighborly. I see the secrets in their eyes;
all of them as they
gallop through streets cluttered
with the unknown.

Shhhhhh!

Another one is revealed;
another face unveiled from underneath truth
in the recognition of realities capture.
I see the secrets in their eyes; all of them:
strangers, mailmen, acquaintances,
celebrities, parents
and admirers
exposed for their humanity
as *just people*.

Break Of Dawn

My world does not sleep tonight/eyes are opened tight.
My wind is walking recklessly
through elevators of time just to stand still
in the fragments of an imagination
that refuses to escape an awakened dream
where everything appears just as they seem

I am a poet; an observer disguised as an insomniac
with thoughts trampling my sleep
into a temple of desire chained closed
against my entrance and the capitalization of my existence
 so I stand outside banging
on the unanswered doors that shelter my rest,

but my alert digestion refuses to unlock
the endless aggression of the mind/calmness left behind;
now the hours are exploding into another day
leaving me reluctantly awake in the distance
where dreams fail to exist and restlessness
is embodying the break of dawn.

VII. The Adventures Of Mr. Poetry

"I am looking for a poem that says Everything so I don't have to write anymore." ~Tukaram

Mr .Poetry I

I saw a poem…

and he was standing on the corner
of Main street dressed in euphony;
a rugged gentleman with a tilted
hat and suspenders holding up
his extended metaphors
with a steady flowing ink dripping
from his pores.

His smile didn't rhyme
with his eyes, but all the same
he flowed in meter with many
meanings to be told, but
with much to withhold he
flattered his admirers with a glimpse
of symbolism while the ambiguity
of his stature echoed in poetic diction.

He danced to the nature
of assonance as leaves floated
from the swaying of the trees
and in an haiku he shared his life
wilting down upon his knees.
He whispered a sweet melody of love
in a sonnet as he spoke
to the heavens above.

He showed many interpretations
as he stood,
                       a poem;

                                        and I called him "Mr. Poetry"

all there on one page to be read
at least that's what he said.

Mr. Poetry II

I saw a poem...

           and he was standing on the corner
of Maple Street waving his fists at honking
traffic reading his lines.

    In fact

He's there all the time, but that day
I just happened to watch his words; words
that didn't speak but resonated
in iambic pentameter
as ink rained down in verses.
Not the typical kind of poem
I usually stop and watch but he captured
me with the ambiguity of his stature

much to be interpreted

Indeed

He symbolized life, but his clothes
didn't rhyme; they stood as one
big stanza of rags hanging
as metaphors twisted and tucked
in by many meanings and aspects of life.

It didn't take much translation
as his eyes reflected those
of Etheridge Knight, a man "born in Mississippi"
who walked 'barefoot thru the mud and born
black in Mississippi'.
And like Mr. Knight

he had a story to tell as he still
walked barefoot,
but on his own will.

And he tracked footprints of inspiration

capturing my admiration

as he was just being himself…a poem
whom I called Mr. Poetry.

Mr. Poetry III

So I saw this poem sitting on a park bench
under a birch tree; a beautiful foliage of changing words
barely holding on with the strong winds of alliteration
blowing wildly as branches danced to the metrical pattern
of the early autumn air.

And he breathed it all in as he sat,

this poem;

a man with hidden meaning teasing me with wordplay
as if he knew I was reading.
I tried not to stare with analytical eyes,
But I liked the way his clothes were written
And the way his movements
shifted like a sestina: a repetition
of stretches and shifts that stood on their own
in meaning.

My interpretation told me he was *waiting*

and the roam of his eyes were relating
to a bit of prose that fell out of his mind;
a picture
that held in a moment of writer's block,
      and he cried
as the words begin to fall from the birch
sprinkling him with soft touches of September
as he remembered
the last time he smiled.

He wasn't hard to translate because he was
the symbolism of lost love

and remembrance; with his soft versed
sweater, lightly rhetoric kangol cap

what he was *waiting* for was the memory

that blew back into his mind; that photograph
of framed poetics that reminded him
of the day his heart changed into the season
of heartbreak.

He was the kind of poem you felt
through the emotion he wrote
his tears in; tears that told a story

with no punctuation.

and he exhaled it all out as he sat

a poem of life.

Mr. Poetry IV

I lost my eyes somewhere between Columbus Ave
and Longhill Street on a blinding Saturday afternoon
in the middle of November.

> The snarling glare from the descending sun spotlighted
> his existence as he mirrored a stubborn traffic
> that growled rolled eyes at the sight of his

> *poetics.*

He was a poem that found my vision
and returned my eyes to a reality I ignored

> until that day.

He was more than just the words:

> *'will work for food'*

Words scribbled on a portion of card board
cut from the material of his shelter; a temporary
shield from the harsh air of cold stares.

> His faded camouflaged jacket

decorated with the American symbol of pride
told the story of a soldier forgotten
and spit on by the country he lost his left leg
for; barely standing and barely recognized,
he was misread in translation of the complexity

> of his struggle.

And I sat there watching his courage
on the battlegrounds of hunger; a veteran
driven by as if he was a bother but yet thankful

      for the one car that stopped and greeted

his heart. He was thankful for being given
a moment of recognition and thankful
for being shown that he did matter in a place

      he called home.

I was thankful for being able to see
life through his eyes as he was a poem
often unread

but on this day

      he was my symbol of inspiration.

Mr. Poetry V

He was a bundle of words broken down
on the side of an unpaved road with nowhere to go.

His eyes were two spirals of stressed syllables
as he wilted down into a Rondeau of repetitive
lines that defined the contradiction of his body language
        as he roadblock/ed his own expression.

The verb verse of his clothes was crying, trying, but dying;
        pretending, descending and defending
all that was written
        and all that he loved but kept layered
in the deep phrases of thought.

        He attacked time by standing still
in fast moving traffic that drifted with no punctuation/
        unedited
with lower case letters of procrastination
that mapped his circle around writer's block;
a block he couldn't seem to unravel
        because he was lost and traveling

with too many commas; too many pauses
        in a stanza that just needed a conjunction
to transition his emotion.

He was that conjunction stuck in the quicksand
of his own ink putting off his chance to get out
        by ignoring the ropes of his own mind
tugging to lift him out of his own
        plagiarism.

He was a lazy poem that could've
            been revised into so much more
if only he wasn't holding back the translation
of his own heart.

Mr. Poetry VI

He sits in his silver 2008 Audi outback, driver side
window half way down, staring off into a sunset
      that rises behind the shadows of existence.
He pretends not to be a poem as he hides
his eyes behind sunglasses but his mind is running
on empty fuels like a car that has been
totaled into a piece of tin just sitting in a junkyard
      empty of acceleration.

The world around him has left him behind
      as he is still stuck in a traffic of self-pity.
Many stanzas have gone wrong in his life/this life
and everything that he has sacrificed
has been rear ended by a lonely moment of road rage
that has become the simile of his soul,
the metaphor of his state of mind
      too hard to hide and too strong
to leave behind.

He turns the ignition to his heart one more time
and again it stalls as his anger roars
      into a desperate cry to rhetoric fumes;
an exhaustion that pollutes the air with everything
he use to be but can never be again.

He is a poem/a tragic poem captured by the headlights
of his own life; stepping endlessly on the petal
of memories that refuse to speed
because everything that he needs
      he lost on the highway of depression.
He drove by every love and every romance
that tried to heal him. Now he no longer believes
in the evolution of the sonnet

       because it has driven him mad
and has him afraid to let go of the brakes
of his freedom to feel again.

He turns the ignition again and his heart
       begins to start as he recognizes
that passion may be within miles if he drives
within the speed limit of his readiness.
He takes off the sunglasses and rolls up the windows
       the tires begin to turn
as he becomes a poem again
       driving to find the simple meaning
in the complexity of an emotion   like a haiku.

Mr. Poetry VII

He leaned against the brick wall of prose
    as a pose
dialing the syllables to another stanza
of an epistle that captured his every second,
minute, moment and verse of thought.

He was waiting,

        but he loved her too much

which caused a translation that yielded him to hesitate
speaking her name, there in the silence, in a subway
station with no rhythm to his heart and no meter
to the pulse of the hurt he caused.

        So there he was, a poem, waiting…

waiting for the right words to write with his voice;
waiting for just the right pronunciation towards forgiveness;
waiting for the courage to plead the complications
that his metrical pattern has in the form of his mistakes.

        Their life together was an Otava Rima: A free flowing
expression of love and dedication but it was the line
that didn't rhyme that tore them apart and led him their
with no more excuses because within the acrostic
of her tears he knew he ruined the structure

by offsetting the diction of commitment.
And one last dial was interrupted

        by the train pulling in. It was his time to go
and before three rings he hung up
as a means of giving up.

There was no more changes,
                                he waited too long.

Mr. Poetry VIII

There was something about the way his eyes rhymed
that made me recognize him as a poem. He had a deep
stare traveling a road leading to nowhere, eyes
       searching for the right path
to lead him to somewhere as he/ was a stanza lost
in the translation of life; a quatrain left to stand alone
with just enough lines left in his heart
       to make him believe he had a meaning.

Fourteen years old and left behind feeling forgotten, his search
for a new tomorrow seemed like endless steps
down an empty road of beaten dirt and emotional
weeds battered enough
       to leave the scars of abuse
layered on the skin of his mind. His soul
was a runaway teenager written in an acrostic:

       Hoping to find healing,
       Exploring for an answer,
       Learning to feel his own voice, and
       Pleading not to feel the hurt inside…

any longer.

 He was on the road often traveled by the scents of poetry
       escaping the genre
of child abuse as he had to become a man
before his growth had a chance to adjust to the ambiguities
of adolescence, but he found the symbolism
in his own alliteration

       finding freedom from fear,

and recognized the irony in the spoken word
beating through the microphone of a poem left unwanted;
he had a voice that was very much needed
      on a road where many children of abuse
were crying the same ink.

I saw at first as a euphony of sadness but the more I read
the more I interpreted a ballad with more to be written
      as his life was just beginning.
He had no one but had the hands of everyone
guiding him down that lonely road to a new destination
known as the ode of survival.

Would you like to see your manuscript become a book?

If you are interested in becoming a PublishAmerica author, please submit your manuscript for possible publication to us at:

acquisitions@publishamerica.com

You may also mail in your manuscript to:

**PublishAmerica
PO Box 151
Frederick, MD 21705**

www.publishamerica.com

PublishAmerica

CPSIA information can be obtained at www.ICGtesting.com
Printed in the USA
LVOW07s1417241115

464023LV00001B/19/P

9 781462 654390